The People's Right of Local, Community Self-Government:

Grant Township v. Pennsylvania General Energy Company

GRANT TOWNSHIP'S MEMORANDUM IN SUPPORT OF ITS MOTION FOR JUDGMENT ON THE PLEADINGS

The Community Environmental Legal Defense Fund
Pennsylvania

The Community Environmental Legal Defense Fund
P.O. Box 360
Mercersburg, Pennsylvania, USA 17236
www.celdf.org

ISBN #978-1-312-89350-4

Text and cover design by the Community Environmental Legal Defense
Fund

Dedicated to
Judy, Stacy, J.P., Mark, Bill, Fred, Sue, Mona, and the People of
Grant Township, Indiana County, Pennsylvania.

Special thanks to
Ben, Chad, Lindsey, and the rest of the staff of the Community
Environmental Legal Defense Fund who make this work possible.

Preface:

A Rural Community Defends Itself from Oil and Gas Waste

Faced with plans by an oil and gas company to inject fracking waste into their Township - along with the issuance of state and federal permits approving that injection - the people of rural Grant Township, Indiana County, Pennsylvania decided that enough was enough.

They approached the Community Environmental Legal Defense Fund, a law firm specializing in assisting communities to stop harmful corporate projects, about drafting a local law that would protect their community from the dumping of oil and gas wastes.

On June 3, 2014, the people of Grant Township and their local elected officials adopted Grant's Community Bill of Rights Ordinance. The Ordinance created a local bill of rights for the people and ecosystems of the Township, banned activities that would violate those rights, and removed competing "rights" claimed by corporations and other business entities that would interfere with those rights.

On August 12, 2014, the Pennsylvania General Energy Company, LLC sued Grant Township in federal court, seeking a ruling that the Ordinance was unconstitutional and illegal. In response, the people of Grant counter-sued the company, claiming that the company was violating their right of local, community self-government. This book consists of the brief filed by the people of Grant in defense of their Ordinance.

The Right of Local, Community Self-Government: An Inherent Right Reborn

This legal brief explains how the right of local, community self-government is not a new right. It argues that the right is a natural, inherent, and inalienable right belonging to the people, and that it is recognized by the history of the founding of this country, the Declaration of Independence, state constitutions, and the U.S. Constitution.

Although being one of the most ancient of rights, our current legal system does not recognize that right and thus, does not protect it. Instead, the current system enables certain legal doctrines to override the right. Those doctrines include corporations possessing constitutional "rights," state and federal preemption – in which state and federal laws automatically override conflicting local ones – and "Dillon's Rule," in which our local communities are wholly controlled by state governments.

This legal brief explains why and how those doctrines are incompatible with the people's exercise of their right of local, community self-government, and therefore, why those doctrines must give way to that right.

Rights of Natural Communities and Ecosystems

In addition to recognizing the people's right of local, community self-government, Grant's Ordinance recognizes that the injection of frack wastes into the Township would be harmful not just to the people of Grant, but also to the natural environment. To protect the natural environment, the Ordinance establishes that natural communities and ecosystems possess rights of their own – to "exist, flourish, and naturally evolve."

Grant's Ordinance reflects a frustration with current environmental laws, which are focused more on permitting and legalizing certain corporate activities than on protecting the natural environment. Therefore, the Ordinance recognizes that ecosystems have rights, protects those ecosystems from activities that would violate those rights, and recognizes that the people of Grant may defend those rights in the name of the ecosystem. The Ordinance is part of a larger movement towards the recognition of a rights-based system of environmental protection – one that now includes several dozen communities in the United States adopting laws recognizing the rights of nature.

The Path Ahead

The people of Grant understand that they are part of a growing movement in the United States toward elevating the rights of communities above the "rights" of corporations and other business entities. They understand that courts may or may not find their arguments persuasive, but that in the end, both state and federal constitutional structures must change to protect the rights of their community and nature. Their adoption of the Grant Ordinance is part of that movement.

Over the past ten years, close to two hundred communities in ten states have adopted similar laws. With the help of the Community Environmental Legal Defense Fund, communities in those states have joined together to create state-level Community Rights Networks, and those coalitions have now joined together to create the National Community Rights Network. Both the state-level networks and the federal one are focused on driving state and federal constitutional change that finally recognizes and enforces the people's right of local, community self-government and the rights of nature.

In the United States District Court
for the Western District of Pennsylvania

PENNSYLVANIA GENERAL
ENERGY COMPANY, L.L.C.

        Plaintiff,

vs.

GRANT TOWNSHIP,

        Defendant.

)
)
)
)
)
)
)
)
)
)
)
)

No. 1:14-cv-209

J. Frederick Motz, J.

Electronically Filed

GRANT TOWNSHIP'S MEMORANDUM IN SUPPORT OF ITS MOTION FOR JUDGMENT ON THE PLEADINGS

For Defendant Grant Township
Thomas Alan Linzey, Esq.
Community Environmental Legal Defense Fund
P.O. Box 360
Mercersburg, Pennsylvania 17236
(717) 498-0054 (v)

TABLE OF CONTENTS

Appendix: The Grant Township Community Bill of Rights Ordinance

I.   SUMMARY OF THE ARGUMENT

The right of local, community self-government is a fundamental, individual political right – exercised collectively – of people to govern the local communities in which they reside.

The right includes three component rights – first, the right to a system of government within the local community that is controlled by a majority of its citizens; second, the right to a system of government within the local community that secures and protects the civil and political rights of every person in the community; and third, the right to alter or abolish the system of local government if it infringes those component rights.

The right of local, community self-government is inherent and inalienable. It derives necessarily from the fundamental principle that *all* political power is inherent in the people, is exercised by them for their benefit, and is subject to their control. The right is secured by the Pennsylvania Constitution, the American Declaration of Independence, state constitutional bills of rights, and the United States Constitution. Because the right is inherent and inalienable, no government can define, diminish, or otherwise control it.

State governments have created a variety of local governmental bodies, both incorporated and unincorporated, for administration of state policy locally, and for conduct of municipal affairs. While States typically delegate specific governmental powers to such local governments - and limit their powers otherwise - state authorized powers of such local governments are distinct and apart from the people's right of local, community self-government. The peoples' right is not dependent upon state delegation, and so, cannot be diminished by limitations placed on local governments by other governments.

This means that local communities, when exercising the people's right of local, community self-government, are not subject to constraints on local lawmaking imposed by state and federal governments. Such constraints include preemption of local lawmaking by state and federal laws or international treaties; the conferral of constitutional rights onto corporations, when those "rights" compete with people's civil and political rights; and the doctrine that local governments can legislate only as authorized by state government.

II. FACTUAL AND PROCEDURAL HISTORY

Grant Township is a small, rural community of seven hundred residents. Pennsylvania General Energy Company, LLC ("PGE") currently operates natural gas wells within the Township, including a deep gas well on property known as the Yanity Farm (hereinafter "Yanity Well"). The company is currently seeking to convert that existing deep gas well to an injection well – thus enabling it to inject waste fluids and brine produced by fracking and other oil and gas extraction activities. [Doc. 5 at ¶¶ 18-28].

The people of Grant Township, and the Grant Township Board of Supervisors, do not want oil and gas waste materials injected into land within their community. [Doc. 1-1 at ¶ 2]. They fear that injecting waste materials from oil and gas extraction has the potential to contaminate their water and otherwise adversely affect the health, safety, and welfare of the residents and their community.[1] They believe that the relevant state and federal regulatory agencies are more interested in issuing permits to allow the injection to occur, than in protecting the people and natural environment of Grant Township. *Id.* at ¶¶ 2-3.

On June 3, 2014, the people of Grant Township, through their municipal elected officials, adopted a Community Bill of Rights Ordinance [hereinafter "Ordinance"] [Doc. 1-1]. That Ordinance establishes a local bill of rights and then prohibits those activities – like the depositing of oil and gas waste materials into the Township – that would violate those rights. The local bill of rights recognizes the rights of residents to clean air, clean water, and a sustainable energy future. [Doc. 1-1 (Ordinance at §2)] (codifying the "right to clean air, water, and soil;" the "right to scenic preservation;" and the "right to a sustainable energy future").

The Ordinance also recognizes that the people of the Township have a federal, state, and locally-secured constitutional right to govern their own community. That right – the right of local, community self-government - includes the right to change their municipal system of governance if it has been rendered incapable of either protecting their civil and political rights, or of recognizing the authority of a community majority to make governing decisions for the locality. [Doc. 1-1 (Ordinance at §2(a) (recognizing and securing the "right to local self-government"))].

In response to the adoption of the Community Bill of Rights Ordinance by the people and elected officials of Grant Township, PGE sued the Township on August 12, 2014. [Doc. 1]. The thirteen count amended complaint seeks to nullify Grant's Ordinance based on three categories of claims – the first alleges that the Ordinance violates corporate constitutional "rights," [Doc. 5 at Counts I-VI], the second alleges that the Township lacked the authority to adopt the Ordinance pursuant to the doctrine of "Dillon's Rule," [Doc. 5 at Count VII], and the third alleges that certain state laws preempt the Ordinance [Doc. 5 at Counts VIII-XI]. In its amended complaint, PGE added a Sunshine Act claim to the original counts – alleging that the Township failed to hold a public vote on retaining a law firm to defend the municipality in this action. [Doc. 5 at Count XII].

In its Answer, the Defendant filed a Counterclaim against the Plaintiff, asserting that the Plaintiff's action violates the right of the people of Grant Township to local, community self-government. [Doc. 10 at 18-30]. The Plaintiff has filed an Answer to that Counterclaim. [Doc. 22]. The Defendant now files this motion for judgment on the pleadings, asking this Court to grant its motion, dismiss this case, and find PGE liable for the violation of the rights of the Defendant and the people of Grant Township.

III. STANDARD FOR JUDGMENT ON THE PLEADINGS AND FOR LIABILITY UNDER 42 U.S.C. §1983

Rule 12(c) motions for judgment on the pleadings are judged according to the same standard that applies to 12(b)(6) motions to dismiss. *Gebhart v. Steffen*, 574 Fed.Appx. 156, 158 (3d Cir. 2014) (citing *Turbe v. Gov. of Virgin Islands*, 938 F.2d 427, 428 (3d Cir.1991)).

When considering a motion to dismiss, the court accepts all of the opposing parties' "factual allegations as true [and] construe[s] the complaint in the light most favorable" to that party. *Byers v. Intuit, Inc.*, 600 F.3d 286, 291 (3d Cir. 2010). However, a claim must contain "more than labels and conclusions" or a "formulaic recitation of the elements of a cause of action." *Bell Atl. Corp. v. Twombly*, 550 U.S. 544, 555, 127 S.Ct. 1955, 167 L.Ed.2d 929 (2007). To survive a motion to dismiss, "[t]he plaintiff must allege 'enough facts to state a claim to relief that is plausible on its face.'" *Connelly v. Steel Valley Sch. Dist.*, 706 F.3d 209, 212 (3d Cir.2013) (quoting *Twombly*, 550 U.S. at 570, 127 S.Ct. 1955). This standard is not a probability requirement but the plaintiff needs to show "more than a sheer possibility that a defendant has acted unlawfully." *Ashcroft v. Iqbal*, 556 U.S. 662, 678, 129 S.Ct. 1937, 173 L.Ed.2d 868 (2009).

"To state a claim under § 1983, a party must allege the violation of a right secured by the Constitution and laws of the United States, and must show that the alleged deprivation was committed by a person acting under color of state law." *Harvey v. Plains Tp. Police Dept.*, 421 F.3d 185, 189 (3d Cir. 2005) (*quoting West v. Atkins*, 487 U.S. 42, 48 (1988)). A showing that the party used some state-derived authority to cause the alleged harm is sufficient to show state action. *See Abbott v. Latshaw*, 164 F.3d 141,146 (3d Cir.1998).

ARGUMENT

IV. **Defendant is entitled to judgment on the pleadings because the people of Grant Township possess the inherent and constitutional right of local, community self-government, and legal doctrines asserted by PGE in this action violate that right.**

The people of Grant Township's natural, inherent, and inalienable right of local, community self-government is embedded in, and secured by, our constitutional structure.[2] *See Indiana ex rel. Holt v. Denny*, 118 Ind. 449, 457-75, 21 N.E. 274 (1889) (recognizing an inherent right of local self-government embedded in the constitutional structure). It is secured by the history of the founding of the United States, the American Declaration of Independence, the U.S. Constitution, the Pennsylvania Constitution, and the Grant Township Ordinance.

The constitutional right of the people of Grant Township to govern themselves is infringed by the legal doctrines asserted by PGE in this action – the existence and enforcement of corporate constitutional "rights," Dillon's Rule, and the related doctrine of preemption (when preemption is applied to set a ceiling, rather than a floor, for local lawmaking that secures the rights of community members). Because PGE seeks to enforce those doctrines in ways which violate the constitutional right of the people of Grant Township to local, community self-government, the Defendant is entitled to judgment on the pleadings.

A. Community self-government is the well-settled foundation of the American system of constitutional law.

The Supreme Court has declared that "when considering whether a right is a fundamental right, the court [must] look to whether it is a right "deeply rooted in this nation's history and tradition." *Griswold v. Connecticut*, 381 U.S. 479, 493 (1965) (Brennan, J., concurring) (courts look

8

to "traditions and (collective) conscience of our people to determine whether a principle is so rooted" there "as to be ranked as fundamental.") (citations omitted); *Moore v. City of East Cleveland*, 431 U.S. 494, 503 (1997) ("Appropriate limits on substantive due process come not from drawing arbitrary lines but rather from careful 'respect for the teachings of history (and), solid recognition of the basic values that underlie our society'") (*quoting Griswold*, 381 U.S. at 501 (Harlan, J., concurring)).

The right of community self-governance is deeply rooted in our nation's history and tradition. Communities within the early American colonies were founded on the people's authority to govern themselves. From the Mayflower Compact to the conflagration of the American Revolutionary War and the ratification of the United States Constitution, no principle has been more seminal than that of the people's sovereignty, and no right more fundamental than the right of local, community self-government. *Cf. Washington v. Glucksberg*, 521 U.S. 702, 721 (1997) (declaring that "[o]ur Nation's history, legal traditions, and practices thus provide the crucial guideposts for responsible decisionmaking" that direct the court's recognition and enforcement of constitutional guarantees) (citation omitted).

The colonists' struggle with British rule illustrates how community self-government took shape as the foundation of the American system of constitutional law. The colonists' efforts culminated in the Declaration of Independence, which codified the principles of local self-government that had been forged by American settlements since the 1600s. In adopting the Declaration of Independence, in 1776, the Second Continental Congress made clear that a government's power originates from the people, and that the people have the right to alter their system of government to protect their "Life, Liberty . . . Safety and Happiness":

> We hold these truths to be self-evident, that all men are created equal, that they are endowed by their Creator with certain unalienable Rights, that among these are Life, Liberty and the pursuit of Happiness. — That to secure these rights, Governments are instituted among Men, deriving their just powers from the consent of the governed, — *That whenever any Form of Government becomes destructive of these ends, it is the Right of the People to alter or to abolish it, and to institute new Government, laying its foundation on such principles and organizing its powers in such form, as to them shall seem most likely to effect their Safety and Happiness.*

AMER. DECL.OF IND. at ¶ 2 (emphasis added).

9

The violation of this right, enumerated in the Declaration as the first grievance against the British Empire, justifying severance from its rule, read "HE has refused his Assent to Laws, the most wholesome and necessary for the public Good." *Id.* at ¶ 3. Since there were neither states, nor a national government at the time, the grievance constitutes a complaint against the denial of the colonists' right to local, community self-government.

1. **Community self-government was the foundation of the early American colonies.**

The concept of community self-government in America dates back to the Mayflower Compact, adopted in 1620, over a hundred and fifty years before Thomas Jefferson codified the principles of local self-government in the national Declaration of Independence.[3] The Mayflower Compact was the first constitution of its kind to be written by the American colonists, and it set the stage for an understanding of government that represented a dramatic departure from European rule. In one paragraph, the original colonists dismantled the old system of government—based on royal authority—and forged a new one based purely on the political sovereignty of the people themselves. They declared:

> [W]e covenant and combine ourselves together into a civil body politic, for our better ordering, and preservation, and furtherance of the ends aforesaid; and by virtue hereof to enact, constitute, and frame, such just and equal laws, ordinances, acts, constitutions, and offices, from time to time, as shall be thought most meet and convenient for the general good of the colony.[4]

Far from being unusual, such early American concepts of community self-government—that people possessed the authority to create, control, and change their own governing systems—were the norm. In the 1620s, early colonists founded settlements in New Hampshire that became the Towns of Portsmouth and Dover. Both were "wholly self-ruled," and Dover's inhabitants self-organized themselves into a "body politic … with all such laws as shall be concluded by a major part of the Freemen of our Society." In 1639, the settlers of Exeter, New Hampshire, created their own government, declaring in the Exeter Compact that we "combine ourselves together to erect and set up among us such Government. . . according to the libertyes of our English colony of

Massachusetts." Lutz, ed., COLONIAL ORIGINS OF THE AMERICAN CONSTITUTION: A DOCUMENTARY HISTORY 3 (1998).

People in towns, villages, and colonies also joined with people from other areas to create broader levels of government to further secure their right to community self-government. For example, on January 14, 1639, people from the Connecticut Towns of Windsor, Hartford, and Wethersfield joined together to adopt the Fundamental Orders of Connecticut, the first written state constitution in America, which created a compact securing the right of self-government within those Towns.[5] And in 1643, the people of various towns and colonies joined together to create the United Colonies of New England, approving Articles of Confederation for the United Colonies which declared that the people of each plantation, town, and colony shall have "exclusive jurisdiction and government within their limits," thereby securing their authority to self-govern locally.[6]

Judge Eugene McQuillan, author of a seminal treatise on the law of municipal corporations, explained that those communities constituted "miniature commonwealths. . . [with] the solid foundation of that well-compacted structure of self-government." McQuillan, A TREATISE ON THE LAW OF MUNICIPAL CORPORATIONS, Vol. 1 at 144 (1911). Thus, the early American colonies were replete with constitutions, compacts, and agreements reflecting that uniquely self-organizing American form of government, one in which the people of those communities possessed the unabridged (and sovereign) right to create, control, and change their systems of governance.[7] Id. at 384–85 ("[T]he people of the various organized communities exercise their rights of local self-government under the protection of these fundamental principles which were accepted, without doubt or question. . .").

2. Community self-government is the foundation of American constitutional law.

While Great Britain tolerated the colonists' self-rule in the interests of efficiency, it believed that final authority over governing matters lie with the British king and parliament. Clashes between these two theories of government—of the right of the American people to create, manage, and alter their systems of government as they saw fit; and the "right" of the British government to manage the colonies—were commonplace in the period leading up to the Revolutionary War.[8] Such clashes led to the development of the doctrine of community self-government as constitutional law, and, inevitably, to revolutionary conflict.

In 1760, colonial lawyer James Otis, Jr. first used the right of community self-government as a constitutional doctrine when he represented colonial merchants in a direct challenge to Great Britain's authority to adopt "writs of assistance". Miller, ORIGINS OF THE AMERICAN REVOLUTION 46 (1962). The writs allowed British authorities to enter any colonist's residence without advance notice or probable cause. Otis argued that the writs were invalid because they had been adopted only by the British parliament, and not by the people of the colonies. Otis' thesis—that the people themselves were the only rightful lawmaking authority—was the first articulation of community self-government as a legal and constitutional doctrine within the colonial context. Beach, SAMUEL ADAMS: THE FATEFUL YEARS 1764-1776 55 (1965). Otis' work, entitled *The Rights of the British Colonies Asserted and Proved,* placed the right of local self-government (including the right to alter any system of governance that undermines that right) at the heart of the patriots' struggle. In his pamphlet he explained:

> There is no one act which a government can have a right to make that does not tend to the advancement of the security, tranquility, and prosperity of the people.... The form of government is by nature and by right so far left to the individuals of each society that they may alter it from a simple democracy or government of all over all to any other form they please....

See Kurland and Lerner, eds., THE FOUNDERS' CONSTITUTION, Vol. 1, Chap. 13, Doc. 4 (1987).

3. Denial of the right of community self-government was the cause of the American Revolution.

The British parliament's denial of the right of local, community self-government was the cause of the American Revolution. In Boston, which would become the epicenter of the American Revolution, a concerted movement—to replace British rule with a system of governance premised on community self-government—began in 1764. That year, the British parliament passed the Currency Acts to remove colonial legislative control over issuing currency. In response, the people of the Town of Boston, through their Town Meeting[9], voted to establish the first, temporary Committee of Correspondence. The Committee was tasked with informing the public about the Currency Acts, along with building public support for repeal. Maier, FROM RESISTANCE TO REVOLUTION 216 (1972). Other towns formed similar committees. *See* Miller, ORIGINS OF THE AMERICAN REVOLUTION 124-26 (1962).

"Stamp Act Riots" against British authority ensued. In 1765, the Stamp Act Congress issued a "Declaration of Rights and Grievances," which focused on the Currency and Stamp Acts' violation of the colonial right to local self-government. The Stamp Act Congress argued that the Currency Act's removal of monetary policy from the colonists, and the Stamp Act's removal of tax policy, violated the people's right of local self-government. *See* JOURNAL OF THE FIRST CONGRESS OF THE AMERICAN COLONIES 29-31 (1845).

The British Parliament retaliated by adopting the "American Colonies Act," which rejected the colonists' authority to self-govern locally. It proclaimed that Parliament "had hath, and of right ought to have, full power and authority to make laws and statutes of sufficient force and validity to bind the colonies and people of America . . . in all cases whatsoever." Maier, FROM RESISTANCE TO REVOLUTION 145 (1972). In response, the colonists attacked the Act as "inconsistent with the natural, constitutional and charter rights and privileges of the inhabitants of this colony." Kruman, BETWEEN AUTHORITY AND LIBERTY: STATE CONSTITUTION MAKING IN REVOLUTIONARY AMERICA 12 (1997).

Over the next decade, Parliament continued to assert taxation authority over the colonists, and the American people continued to assert their right of community self-governance. In 1772, the people of Boston voted to establish the first permanent Committee of Correspondence in the colonies, tasking it with proclaiming "the rights of the colonists. . . [and] to communicate and publish the same to the several towns in this province and to the world as the sense of this town." Miller, ORIGINS OF THE AMERICAN REVOLUTION 329-30 (1962). People in hundreds of towns and villages formed committees to coordinate responses to Parliamentary actions. *Id.*

Also in 1772, frontier settlers living along the Watauga and Nolichucky Rivers, in the eastern part of what would become the state of Tennessee, joined together to become the Watauga Association—the first independent constitutional government in America. After negotiating a ten-year lease with the Cherokee, the settlers unanimously adopted the Articles of the Watauga Association, establishing a local government system, a five member court, a courthouse, and a jail. President Theodore Roosevelt declared that "the Watauga settlers outlined in advance the nation's work. They bid defiance to outside foes and they successfully solved the difficult problem of self-government." Dickinson, "Watauga Association," TENNESSEE ENCYCLOPEDIA OF HISTORY AND CULTURE (2002).

In May 1773, Parliament adopted the Tea Act, allowing the East India Company to sell, for the first time, surplus tea directly to people in the colonies. Purchase of the English tea, and the payment of parliamentary taxes along with it, was viewed as an effort to weaken colonial opposition to parliamentary taxation, and thus to weaken colonial claims to the right of local self-government. Maier, FROM RESISTANCE TO REVOLUTION 275-78 (1972). But the colonists rebelled, resulting in the Boston Tea Party, as well as similar Tea Parties hosted by the people of other towns and villages.

To punish the colonists for their opposition to the Tea Act, Parliament adopted a series of laws known as the "Intolerable Acts" or "Coercive Acts." These sought to nullify completely certain types of colonial self-government.[10] For instance, the British-imposed Massachusetts Government Act sent a clear signal that Great Britain would not tolerate local self-government in the colonies. Miller, ORIGINS OF THE AMERICAN REVOLUTION 369-70 (1962). Long seen as a model for local, community self-government, Massachusetts law had given people wide latitude to make local governing decisions.[11]

The goal of the Massachusetts Government Act was to displace the various legislative mechanisms of local self-government by expanding the royal governor's powers. British officials believed that their inability to control the people of Massachusetts was directly attributable to the highly independent nature of its local governments and the operation of the Town Meeting at the community level. The Act required that each "agenda item at every town meeting in Massachusetts. . . be submitted in writing to the governor and meet with his approval. . . No meeting could be called without the prior consent of the governor." Raphael, THE FIRST AMERICAN REVOLUTION BEFORE LEXINGTON AND CONCORD 50 (2011). As Lord North explained to Parliament, the purpose of the Act was "to take the executive power from the hands of the democratic part of government." Christie and Labaree, EMPIRE OR INDEPENDENCE, 1760-1776 188 (1976). The royal governor eventually used the Act to dissolve the Massachusetts Assembly completely.

14

The people of Massachusetts rebelled against this threat to their right of local self-government by closing down the British judicial system, so that it could not be used to enforce the Act. People in the Towns of Worcester, Springfield, Southampton, Salem, Marblehead, Taunton, and Stoughton not only forcibly closed the courts, but forced hundreds of British officials to resign their positions. Without the courts, the people of those Towns drew up their own plans for keeping order, while urging the people of their own Town Meetings to "pay no regard to the late act of parliament, respecting the calling of town meetings, but, to proceed in their usual manner." Raphael, THE FIRST AMERICAN REVOLUTION BEFORE LEXINGTON AND CONCORD 107 (2011).

> ### 4. Community self-government is the foundation of the Declaration of Independence.

Beginning in 1773, in response to those royal assertions of power and nullification of local self-governance, the people of ninety towns, villages, and counties across the thirteen colonies began to issue their own local declarations of independence. Declaring that only their own homegrown, democratically-elected governments could "constitutionally make any laws or regulations," those communities proclaimed their own independence from British rule years before issuance of a national Declaration of Independence by Congress. Maier, AMERICAN SCRIPTURE: MAKING THE DECLARATION OF INDEPENDENCE 48-49 (1997). The Charlotte Town Resolves, as one example of many, declared in May 1775, over a year before the national declaration, that "all laws derived from the authority of the King or Parliament are annulled and vacated."[12]

It was amidst the issuance of these local declarations that the colonists formed the First Continental Congress, which met in September of 1774, with representatives attending from twelve of the thirteen colonies. During that Congress, the delegates declared: "[a]ssemblies have been frequently dissolved, contrary to the rights of the people … [and] that the inhabitants of the English Colonies in North America, by the immutable laws of nature … are entitled to life, liberty, and property, and they have never ceded to any sovereign power whatever a right to dispose of either without their consent." This articulation of the right of community self-government continued to lay the foundation for the final break between the American colonies and Great Britain.

In May 1776 – before the issuance of the national Declaration of Independence - the Second Continental Congress adopted a resolution that power be transferred from governments resting on the Crown's sovereignty to those based upon popular authority and self-government. The preamble demanded "that the exercise of every kind of authority under the. . . Crown should be totally suppressed." JOURNALS OF THE CONTINENTAL CONGRESS, 4:342, 357-58. Several months later, the people of Virginia adopted the first "Declaration of Rights," which set forth the constitutional doctrine of local self-government:

> Section 2. That all power is vested in, and consequently derived from, the people; that magistrates are their trustees and servants and at all times amenable to them.

> Section 3. That government is, or ought to be, instituted for the common benefit, protection, and security of the people, nation, or *community*; of all the various modes and forms of government, that is best which is capable of producing the greatest degree of happiness and safety and is most effectually secured against the danger of maladministration. And that, when any government shall be found inadequate or contrary to these purposes, a majority of the *community* has an indubitable, inalienable, and indefeasible right to reform, alter, or abolish it, in such manner as shall be judged most conducive to the public weal.[13]

This fundamental principle of local self-government was recognized and reasserted by the Congress in June 1776, when it issued the national Declaration of Independence. Penned originally by Thomas Jefferson and edited by a congressional committee, the Declaration listed the infringement of local self-government as the primary basis for severance from Great Britain.[14] It codified the principles of local self-government that had been forged by the American colonists starting in the 1600s onward. Drawing on the declarations of towns, villages, colonies, compacts, early constitutions, and the writings of James Otis and others, the Declaration reaffirmed four major principles of law:

> -First, that certain rights—those of life, liberty, safety, and the pursuit of happiness—are natural rights, held by virtue of being human[15];

> -Second, that governments are created to secure those natural rights[16];

> -Third, that each government owes its existence to, and derives its power exclusively from, the community that creates it[17]; and

-Fourth, that when government becomes destructive of the people's natural rights, the people have a right (and duty) to alter or abolish that government and establish new forms.[18]

The Declaration of Independence has been congressionally recognized as an organic, enforceable law of the United States, and so is part of the United States Code. *See* 1 U.S.C. at i-iii. In the words of historian Joshua Miller, the great principles "evoked in the Declaration are autonomy of collectivities, natural rights, and the legitimacy of revolution." *See* Miller, THE RISE AND FALL OF DEMOCRACY IN EARLY AMERICA, 1630-1789 70 (1991).

5. Community self-government is the foundation for state constitutions.

The Constitutions adopted by the people of the colonies—transforming the colonies from chartered corporations into sovereign states—reaffirmed and codified, as the basis for those state governments, the four principles of local self-government asserted by the Declaration of Independence.[19] For instance, in Pennsylvania's Declaration of Rights, incorporated into the Pennsylvania Constitution of 1776, the people declared:

> That all men are born equally free, and independent; and have certain, natural, inherent, and inalienable rights; amongst which are; the enjoying and defending of life and liberty; acquiring, possessing, and protecting property; and pursuing and obtaining happiness and safety.

> That all power being originally inherent in, and consequently derived from, the people; therefore all officers of government, whether legislative, or executive, are their trustees, and servants, and at all times accountable to them.

> That government is, or ought to be, instituted for the common benefit, protection and security of the people, nation, or *community*; and not for the particular emolument or advantage of any single man, family, or set of men, who are a part only of that community; And that the *community* hath an indubitable, unalienable and indefeasible right to reform, alter, or abolish government in such manner as shall be by that *community* judged most conducive to the public weal.[20]

In addition to being expressly secured by state constitutions, the right of community self-government was embodied in the process by which the people of each state drafted and adopted their constitutions. All but one of the thirteen original colonies entrusted the responsibility of drafting new constitutions to the people themselves through constitutional conventions, rather than through permanent state legislatures. *See* Marc Kruman, BETWEEN AUTHORITY AND LIBERTY: STATE CONSTITUTION MAKING IN REVOLUTIONARY AMERICA 157-58 (1997).

6. The Pennsylvania Constitution guarantees the right of local, community self-government to the people of Grant Township.

Pennsylvania's Constitution of 1776 explicitly secured the people's inalienable right to *community* self-government in its formulation of the source and scope of - and manner of altering - governmental authority. It reaffirmed that the people are the source of all governmental power and that governments must exercise that power for the common benefit of people and their *communities*. To ensure that this is so, the *community* has "an indubitable, unalienable and indefeasible right to reform, alter or abolish government."[21]

The history of local government in Pennsylvania at the time shows that the word "community" meant local communities. The members of Pennsylvania's Constitutional Convention of 1776 consisted largely of people who resisted both British rule and the centralization of political power in the City of Philadelphia.[22] Members of the constitutional convention wished to govern themselves locally and be free from both British rule and imperial-style control by the colonial power base in Philadelphia.

Mindful of a potentially oppressive state government, they ensured that Pennsylvania's first constitution emphasized that the right of self-government exists at the local, community level. Accordingly, Pennsylvania has historically recognized that it is the people who give the state the authority to govern and not the other way around. *See People v. Hurlbut*, 24 Mich. 44 (1871) (Cooley, J., concurring) ("[L]ocal government is a matter of absolute right; and the state cannot take it away."); *see also* Thomas M. Cooley, A TREATISE ON THE CONSTITUTIONAL LIMITATIONS WHICH REST UPON THE LEGISLATIVE POWER OF THE STATES OF THE AMERICAN UNION 47 (5th Ed. 1883).

Pennsylvania adopted a second constitution in 1790. The Pennsylvania Constitution of 1790 reaffirmed that people are the source of governmental power and, as such, they have the unalienable and indefeasible right to alter, reform, or abolish their government:

> That the general, great, and essential principles of liberty and free Government may be recognized and unalterably established, WE DECLARE,
>
> Of the origin of power, and the end of government. Section II. That all power is inherent in the people, and all free governments are founded on their authority, and instituted for their peace, safety and happiness: For the advancement of those ends, they have, at all times, an unalienable and indefeasible right to alter, reform, or abolish their government, in such manner as they may think proper.

See PENNSYLVANIA CONSTITUTION OF 1790, Art. IX Declaration of Rights, §II (reprinted in Gormley, THE PENNSYLVANIA CONSTITUTION at 880).

The Pennsylvania Constitution made clear that the people's right of self-government could not be overridden by other levels of government:

> Exception from the general powers of government. Section XXVI. To guard against the transgression of the high powers which we have delegated, WE DECLARE, That everything in this article [on the Declaration of Rights] is excepted out of the general powers of government, and shall for ever remain inviolate.[23]

The exception clause recognizes the truism that the peoples' inherent, inalienable rights are forever superior to the state government established by the constitution, not subject to control by the state government.[24]

All Pennsylvania Constitutions since that of 1790, including the current Pennsylvania Constitution, have contained, in the Declaration of Rights, both the inalienable right of self-government, and the exception of the right from the general powers of the state government. *See* PENNSYLVANIA CONSTITUTION OF 1838, Art. IX Declaration of Rights, §§II, XXVI (reprinted in Gormley, THE PENNSYLVANIA CONSTITUTION at 884, 887); PENNSYLVANIA CONSTITUTION OF 1874, Art. I Declaration of Rights, §§2, 26 (reprinted in Gormley, THE PENNSYLVANIA CONSTITUTION at 887, 891); PENNSYLVANIA CONSTITUTION OF 1968,

Art. I Declaration of Rights, §§2 ("Reservation of Powers in People"), 25 (reprinted in Gormley, THE PENNSYLVANIA CONSTITUTION at 891, 895).

7. The U.S. Constitution guarantees the right of local, community self-government to the people of Grant Township.

The U.S. Constitution also secures the right of local, community self-government in a number of places. The Preamble says:

> We the People of the United States, in Order to form a more perfect Union, establish Justice, insure domestic Tranquility, provide for the common defence, promote the general Welfare, and secure the Blessings of Liberty to ourselves and our Posterity, do ordain and establish this Constitution for the United States of America.

U.S. CONST. at Preamble.

Three of the four principles of self-government from the Declaration appear here, though more loosely. The words "justice, tranquility, defence, welfare, and blessings of liberty" express the Declaration's principle that people have certain natural rights by virtue of being human. The words "in Order to" and "do ordain and establish" express the Declaration's principle that people form governments to secure their civil and political rights. The words "We the People of the United States" express the Declaration's principle that governmental authority stems from the people of the community exercising the powers of government, and is to be exercised for their benefit only. Only the Declaration's fourth fundamental principle, on the people's authority to alter or abolish governments, fails to find literal expression in the Preamble.[25]

The founders debated whether more explicitly to insert all four principles of the Declaration of Independence directly into the Constitution's preamble, or whether the people's right of self-government was so fundamental that it need not be expressly stated in the text of the Constitution itself.[26] Advocating for express inclusion, James Madison argued: "[i]f it be a truth, and so self-evident that it cannot be denied—if it be recognized, as is the fact in many of the State Constitutions. . . this solemn truth should be inserted in the Constitution."[27]

The House rejected the addition, significantly because it deemed the language already incorporated within the Constitution's preamble. Roger Sherman explained that since:

this right is indefeasible, and the people have recognized it in practice, the truth is better asserted than it can be by any words whatever. The words "We the people," in the original Constitution, are as copious and expressive as possible; any addition will only drag out the sentence without illuminating it. . . [28]

Fourteen years later, the U.S. Supreme Court, in *Marbury v. Madison*, 5 U.S. (1 Cranch) 137 (1803), validated Sherman's reasoning. Interpreting the Constitution's preamble as recognizing the people's inherent and fundamental right of self-government, the Court concluded:

> [t]hat the people have an original right to establish, for their future government, such principles as, in their own opinion, shall most conduce to their own happiness, is the basis on which the whole American fabric has been erected.

Marbury, 5 U.S. (1 Cranch) at 176. [29]

The right of local, community self-government, as a fundamental right, is also protected by the Ninth Amendment of the Bill of Rights. That Amendment says: "the enumeration in the Constitution, of certain rights, shall not be construed to deny or disparage other rights retained by the people." As the concurrence in *Griswold*, 381 U.S. at 488, explained: "The language and history of the Ninth Amendment reveal that the Framers of the Constitution believed that there are additional fundamental rights, protected from governmental infringement, [in addition to] those fundamental rights specifically mentioned in the first eight constitutional amendments."

Historical evidence uncovered in the last twenty-five years reinforces that the public intent of this amendment was to elevate the natural rights of people - that pre-existed the Constitution - to the same status, whether or not the rights were explicitly enumerated in the Bill of Rights. Randy E. Barnett, *The Ninth Amendment: It Means What It Says*, 85 TEX. L. REV. 1, 28-29 (2006). These pre-existing natural rights include individual rights as well as collective rights. *Id.* at 21, 20, and 46.

Among the retained rights of the people is the fundamental right to alter or abolish their form of government whenever they see fit. *See* 2 Blackstone's COMMENTARIES: WITH NOTES OF REFERENCE TO THE CONSTITUTION AND LAWS OF THE FEDERAL GOVERNMENT OF THE UNITED STATES AND OF THE COMMONWEALTH OF VIRGINIA 162 (1803); *Deitz v City of Central*, 1 Colo. Rptr. 323 (Colo. Terr. 1871); *Henry Broderick, Inc. v. Riley*,157 P.2d 954, 966 (Wash. 1945) (the Ninth

Amendment serves as a "sentinel against overcentralization of government, [and serves as a] monument to the wisdom of the constitutional framers who realized that for the stable preservation of our form of government, it is essential that local governmental functions be locally performed."). As legal scholar Kurt Lash explains:

> The right to local self-government is a right retained by all people and can be exercised in whatever political direction the people please. What we have forgotten, what we have lost, is that the right to local self-government is more than an idea. It is a right enshrined in the Constitution itself.

Kurt Lash, THE LOST HISTORY OF THE NINTH AMENDMENT 360 (2009).[30]

Accordingly, the people of Grant Township possess an inherent, federal, and state guaranteed right of local, community self-government, secured by the Declaration of Independence, the Pennsylvania Constitution, and the United States Constitution.

8. The Grant Township Ordinance guarantees the right of local, community self-government to the people of Grant Township.

Grant's Community Bill of Rights Ordinance recognizes the federal and state constitutionally-guaranteed right of local, community self-government, while securing that right at the local level. Declaring that the Ordinance was adopted pursuant to the "guarantees of the Declaration of Independence and the United States Constitution," the Ordinance establishes that

> **Right to Local Self-Government**. All residents of Grant Township possess the right to a form of governance where they live which recognizes that all power is inherent in the people and that all free governments are founded on the people's consent.

[Doc. 1-1 (Ordinance at §2(a))].

The doctrines of corporate constitutional "rights," Dillon's Rule (state-delegated limitations on municipal authority), and preemption[31] violate the right to local, community self-government because these doctrines prevent or inhibit the people's ability to exercise that right. Put another way, these doctrines are incompatible with, and therefore violate, the right of local, community self-government. Because these doctrines violate the right of local, community self-government, the Community Rights Ordinance lawfully nullifies them.

B. Corporate constitutional "rights," Dillon's Rule, and the doctrine of preemption all unconstitutionally infringe the people's right of local, community self-government.

Given the colonial history of local self-government in America, the foundation of our state and federal constitutions on local, community self-government, and the now mythic quality attached to the idea of "democracy" here, it is strange that the notion of local communities making decisions with the force of law is so foreign to American jurisprudence. Yet it is.

Community lawmaking as the legitimate exercise of self-government by people *where they live* has generated mostly critical, occasionally derisive treatment from legislators, jurists, and commentators since the time of the founding. Consistent with this attitude, American jurisprudence has developed legal doctrines to infringe the right of local, community self-government, both by denying it outright, and by severely restricting local governmental power allowed for communities by state law. Such doctrines include corporate constitutional "rights," Dillon's Rule, and preemption.

1. The existence and enforcement of corporate constitutional "rights" violates the right of local, community self-government.

One of the doctrines that infringes the right of local, community self-government is that of corporate constitutional "rights." Business corporations are a species of property. The doctrine of corporate constitutional "rights" gives the constitutional rights of people to this property. Then, when local government enacts a law that a corporation dislikes, the corporation may assert its constitutionally-derived "rights" to challenge and defeat the law.[32] Thus, the existence and enforcement of that doctrine prevents the people of Grant Township from exercising their right of local, community self-government.

a. Business corporations are chartered by state governments as subordinate entities.

The cause of the American Revolutionary War was the systemic usurpation of the rights of colonists by the British King and Parliament.[33] Those usurpations occurred largely through the King's empowerment of eighteenth century corporations of global trade, such as the East India Company. Oft-cited as the final spark of the War, the Boston Tea Party was the direct result of colonial opposition to the East India Company's securing of representation for its interests from the British government through the transfer of corporate tariff obligations to the colonists as taxes. This preferential governmental treatment of corporations over people enabled the Company to monopolize the tea market in the colonies while the people's right to representation and local self-government were actively violated.[34]

After the Revolution—and in recognition of their experiences with those British corporations—the colonists placed corporations under strict control. Early legislatures granted charters one at a time, for a limited number of years,[35] held business owners liable for harms and injuries, revoked corporate charters when necessary, forbade banking corporations from engaging in trade, prohibited corporations from owning each other, and established that corporations could only be chartered for "public purposes."[36]

It is well-settled law that business corporations are creations of the state.[37] The United States Supreme Court has repeatedly reaffirmed that business corporations are "creatures" of the state.[38] As such, they are chartered by the state in the name of the people. It also is well-settled law that the Constitution not only protects people against the "State itself," but also against "all of its creatures." *See West Virginia State Board of Education v. Barnette*, 319 U.S. 624, 637 (1943).

b. Over the past 150 years, the judiciary has "found" corporations within the U.S. Constitution and bestowed constitutional rights upon them.

Contrary to the fact that corporations are creatures of the state and thus inferior to the people, over the past 150 years, the judiciary has conferred constitutional rights—once intended to protect only natural persons—upon corporations.[39] It has done so by "finding" corporations in the Fourteenth Amendment[40], the Bill of Rights[41], and the Contracts and Commerce Clauses[42] of the United States Constitution. As the

24

judiciary conferred constitutional rights on corporations, the legal community justified the result with literature on how corporations are legal persons.[43] Nonetheless, the judiciary's finding of corporations within these constitutional guarantees—and especially within the Fourteenth Amendment's guarantees of due process and equal protection—has been challenged by sage Supreme Court jurists.[44]

Recently, Montana Supreme Court Justice James C. Nelson explained well how corporate personhood is a perverted mutation of liberty's roots in natural rights:

> Lastly, I am compelled to say something about corporate "personhood." While I recognize that this doctrine is firmly entrenched in the law, *see Bellotti*, 435 U.S. at 780 n. 15, 98 S. Ct. at 1418 n. 15; *but see* 435 U.S. at 822, 98 S. Ct. at 1439-40 (Rehnquist, J., dissenting), I find the entire concept offensive. Corporations are artificial creatures of law. As such, they should enjoy only those powers—not constitutional rights, but legislatively-conferred powers—that are concomitant with their legitimate function, that being limited-liability investment vehicles for business. Corporations are not persons. Human beings are persons, and it is an affront to the inviolable dignity of our species that courts have created a legal fiction which forces people—human beings—to share fundamental, natural rights with soulless creations of government. Worse still, while corporations and human beings share many of the same rights under the law, they clearly are not bound equally to the same codes of good conduct, decency, and morality, and they are not held equally accountable for their sins. Indeed, it is truly ironic that the death penalty and hell are reserved only to natural persons.

Western Tradition P'ship, Inc. v. Attorney Gen. of State, 271 P.3d 1, 36 (Mont. 2011) (Nelson, J., dissenting), *cert. granted, judgment rev'd sub nom. Am. Tradition P'ship, Inc. v. Bullock*, 132 S. Ct. 2490, 183 L. Ed. 2d 448 (2012).

c. Corporations routinely use constitutional "rights" to deny communities their right of local self-governance.

Endowed by state and federal governments with constitutional rights, business corporations wield those "rights" routinely to override the people's right of local, community self-government. Contemporarily, corporations have used their First[45], Fifth[46], and Fourteenth Amendment "rights" to nullify laws which sought to protect the people's health, safety, and welfare. Corporations have also asserted rights under the Contracts[47] and Commerce[48] Clauses of the U.S. Constitution to strike similar laws.

Efforts to continue to apply corporate constitutional "rights" have been met with increasing resistance in state courts. In 2013, in the Washington County, Pennsylvania Court of Common Pleas in a case dealing with an oil and gas corporation's attempt to shield a settlement agreement from disclosure pursuant to the corporation's Fourth Amendment "rights," President Judge O'Dell-Seneca declared that

> [t]here are no men or women defendants in the instant case; they are various business entities. . . These are all legal fictions, existing not by natural birth but by operations of state statutes. . . Such business entities cannot have been 'born equally free and independent,' because they were not born at all. Indeed, the framers of our constitution could not have intended them to be "free and independent," because, as the creations of the law, they are always subservient to it. . . In the absence of state law, business entities are nothing. Once created, they become property of the men and women who own them, and, therefore, the constitutional rights that business entities may assert are not coterminous or homogenous with the rights of human beings. . .Were they so, the chattel would become the co-equal to its owners, the servant on par with its masters, the agent the peer of its principals, and the legal fabrication superior to the law that created and sustains it. . . They cannot be 'let alone' by government, because businesses are but grapes, ripe upon the vine of the law, that the people of this Commonwealth raise, tend, and prune at their pleasure and need.

Hallowich v. Range Resources Corporation, et al., No. 2010-3954 (Wash. Co. 2013).[49]

In addition to direct infringement of the right of local, community self-government—through the nullification of local and state laws aimed at protecting health, safety, and welfare and other civil and political rights—these assertions of corporate constitutional rights indirectly deny the right of self-government by "chilling" the actions of state and local legislators. For example, when Chemical Waste Management, Inc. successfully sued the State of Alabama on the claim that the State's differential taxation of out-of-state-generated hazardous waste violated the corporation's rights under the Commerce Clause[50], the decision served to eliminate legislative options in all states that sought to protect residents from the influx of out-of-state-generated hazardous waste.

2. Dillon's Rule unconstitutionally infringes on the right of the people of Grant Township to local, community self-government.

Count VII of PGE's amended complaint against Grant Township alleges that the Township acted outside of its authority by enacting the Community Bill of Rights Ordinance. [Doc. 5 at ¶¶ 68-76]. PGE asserts that the Township possesses "only such powers that have been granted to them by the Pennsylvania General Assembly. *Id.* at ¶ 69. In making its claim, PGE relies on a legal doctrine known as "Dillon's Rule," which says that local governments serve at the whim of state legislatures, which have absolute authority to create them, define and limit their powers, and even to eliminate them. *See* John Forrest Dillon, LL.D, COMMENTARIES ON THE LAW OF MUNICIPAL CORPORATIONS, at 154-156 (5th Ed. 1911) ("Municipal corporations owe their origin to, and derive their powers and rights wholly from, the legislature.").

Ironically, it is the same theory of government that was rejected by the colonists in the American Revolution. The British viewed colonial governments as creatures of the crown, serving at the whim of the King, with laws subject to revision or rejection by him.[51] Similarly under Dillon's Rule, local governments – and as a consequence, the people of those municipalities - are merely creatures of the state. It follows that local laws enacted by local governments can only be made pursuant to a power the state allows, and that local laws therefore always remain in danger of being struck.[52]

Judge Eugene McQuillan identified this irony in his 1911 treatise dealing with the law of municipal corporations:

> Among the colonists the creation of government for the management of local concern, in most cases, antedates the establishment of central or state authority. It should be observed, however, it is not the accepted theory in this country that the states have received delegations of power from independent towns; on the other hand, the theory is that the state governments precede the local, create the latter at discretion and endow them with corporate life. But, historically, it is as difficult to prove this theory as it would be to demonstrate that the origin of government is in compact, or that title to property comes from occupancy. The historical fact is, that local governments universally, in this country, were either simultaneous with or preceded the more central authority....

It thus appears that, in this country from the beginning, political power has been exercised by citizens of the various local communities as local communities, and this constitutes the most important feature in our system of government....

Political students at home and abroad have been impressed favorably with our system of local self-government and have regarded it as forming the principle of the life of American liberty throughout our entire national history. In truth, this system constitutes the strength of all free nations. These local organizations enable the people themselves to exercise governmental power in supplying local needs, conveniences and comforts and in regulating the rights of the individual as a component part of the local society in his relations with his neighbors touching public matters....

[F]rom the historical examination of this subject, it becomes manifest that local self-government of the municipality does not spring from nor exist by virtue of written constitutions; that it is not a mere privilege, conferred by the central authority, but that the people in each municipality exercise their franchises under the protection of the fundamental principles just indicated, which were not questioned or doubted when the state constitutions were adopted, and which ... no power in the state can legally disregard.

Eugene McQuillin, A TREATISE ON THE LAW OF MUNICIPAL CORPORATIONS, vol. 1, §§ 62, 69, 70, at 141, 151, 152, 153, 156 (1911) (footnotes omitted).[53]

Pennsylvania jurisprudence has long applied Dillon's Rule to subordinate municipal corporations to the state, and continues to do so today. *See City of Philadelphia v. Fox*, 64 Pa. 169, 180 (Pa. 1870) ("The City of Philadelphia is beyond all question a municipal corporation, that is, a public corporation created by the government for political purposes, and having subordinate and local powers of legislation"); *Naylor v. Township of Hellam*, 565 Pa. 397, 403, 773 A.2d 770, 773 (Pa. 2001) ("Initially, we note that it is fundamental that municipalities are creatures of the state and that the authority of the Legislature over their powers is supreme."); *Huntley & Huntley, Inc., v. Borough Council of Borough of Oakmont*, 600 Pa. 207, 220, 964 A.2d 855, 862 (Pa. 2009) ("Municipalities are creatures of the state and have no inherent powers of their own. Rather, they 'possess only such powers of government as are expressly granted to them and as are necessary to carry the same into effect.'").

In this case, because the Community Bill of Rights Ordinance was adopted *by the people of Grant Township*, Grant Township maintains that Dillon's Rule is inapplicable to the passage of the Ordinance.[54] Even if Dillon's Rule were to apply, it cannot be enforced against the people's right to local, community self-government. *See State v. Hutchinson*, 624 P.2d 1116, 1118-1120 (Utah 1980) ("if there were once valid policy reasons supporting [Dillon's Rule], we think they have largely lost their force and that effective local self-government, as an important constituent part of our system of government, must have sufficient power to deal effectively with the problems with which it must deal."). The people of Grant Township have a constitutional right to self-government in their own community. Dillon's Rule, which requires prior legislative authority for local laws, infringes on that right, and must yield to it.

Under the maxim that people are the source of all political power, it follows that the people must have the inherent and inalienable right to design, administer, and alter local government as they see fit.[55] The people have secured that fundamental right in the Declaration of Independence, the U.S. Constitution, the Pennsylvania Declaration of Rights (specifically at article 1, sections 2 and 25), and now in their Community Bill of Rights Ordinance. The doctrine that the legislature is supreme over local government is, itself, a creature - designed and applied to subvert the fundamental principle that the people of a local community have the sole right and authority to govern themselves.[56]

3. The doctrine of preemption – when applied to set a ceiling, rather than a floor, for local, rights-based lawmaking – violates the constitutional right of the people to local, community self-government.

Counts VIII to XI of PGE's amended complaint against Grant Township assert that the Community Bill of Rights Ordinance is preempted by Pennsylvania's Second Class Township Code [Doc. 5 at ¶¶ 77-82], the Pennsylvania Oil and Gas Act [Doc. 5 at ¶¶ 83-92], the Pennsylvania Municipalities Planning Code [Doc. 5 at ¶¶ 93-97], and the Pennsylvania Limited Liability Company Law [Doc. 5 at ¶¶ 98-102]. In making these assertions, PGE relies on the legal doctrine of preemption, which says that as creatures of the state, local governments may not enact ordinances forbidden by, or in conflict with, federal and state laws and regulations.[57]

Federal and state legislatures often wield preemption expressly, writing into law provisions that prevent local governments from enacting their own laws in particular areas of concern. And even when the legislature does not expressly preempt local regulation, courts can find implied preemption through the judicial doctrines of field and conflict preemption. As explained by the Commonwealth Court of Pennsylvania in *Burkholder v. Zoning Hearing Board*, 902 A.2d 1006 (Pa. Cmwlth 2006):

> The matter of preemption is a *judicially created principle*, based on the proposition that a municipality, as an agent of the state, cannot act contrary to the state. . . In other words, a municipality may be foreclosed from exercising police power it would otherwise have if the Commonwealth has sufficiently acted in a particular field. . . Obviously, local legislation cannot permit what a state statute or regulation forbids or prohibit what state enactments allow.

Burkholder at 1012 (citations omitted) (emphasis added).

Indeed, the Supreme Court of Pennsylvania has declared that preemption bars local lawmaking even if state regulation of the subject area is inadequate. *Harris-Walsh, Inc. v. Borough of Dickson City*, 420 Pa. 262, 274 (1966).

There is a long history of legislative preemption (sometimes explicit, sometimes by judicial interpretation) of local regulation in Pennsylvania. Liquor corporations, mining corporations, banking corporations, oil and gas corporations, agribusiness corporations, timber corporations, development corporations, waste management corporations, and water withdrawal corporations have used the State legislature to preempt community control over a variety of issues.[58]

All of the areas of preemption share one commonality—large economic actors using state law to exempt themselves from local, democratic control. However, even if corporate power were not involved, the doctrine of preemption wrongfully substitutes one government's judgment for another's concerning what is necessary and prudent to protect the civil and political rights of the people of the community. A state government, far removed from the lives and concerns in a community, and influenced by political, social, economic, and fiscal forces beyond the control of that community, tells the community what the people may and may not do governmentally to protect their lives, liberties, safety, and wellbeing.

As argued by Pennsylvania Supreme Court Justice Nigro, in his dissent in *Ortiz v. Commonwealth*, 681 A.2d 152 (Pa. 1996) (preempting

Pennsylvania municipalities from banning assault weapons pursuant to the Pennsylvania Uniform Firearms Act), such control by the state cannot be reconciled with community self-governance:

> In my opinion, whenever the state legislature fails to enact a statute to address a continuing problem of major concern to the citizens of the Commonwealth, a municipality should be *entitled* to enact its own local ordinance in order to provide for the public safety, health, and welfare of its citizens. . .Since Philadelphia County is besieged by a multitude of violent crimes which occur involving a variety of hand guns and automatic weapons it is *fundamentally* essential that the local government enact legislation to protect its citizens whenever the state legislature is unable or unwilling to do so.

Id. at 157 (emphasis in original).

Preemption is not the natural, unavoidable consequence of the state's creation of municipal corporations. When one understands that political power arises only and fully from the people that constitute a government, including a local government, and that they are to exercise that power for their own welfare, free from interference by another government, then one sees how preemption violates the constitutional right of the people to local, community self-government.

C. The people of Grant Township adopted the Community Bill of Rights Ordinance pursuant to their right of local, community self-government, to secure and protect that political right and their civil rights, and to prevent infringement of these rights by corporate constitutional "rights," Dillon's Rule, and the related doctrine of preemption.

By enacting the Community Bill of Rights Ordinance, the people of Grant Township decided that the existing municipal system of law – constrained by precisely the same legal doctrines asserted against the Township by PGE in this action – was failing to provide the most basic constitutional guarantees required of American governments.[59] Those guarantees include the right to governments which recognize the authority of community majorities to govern their own localities, and governments capable of securing and protecting the civil and political rights of the community.

After reaching that realization, the people of Grant Township asserted their constitutionally-embedded right to alter or abolish any system of government which fails to secure those guarantees. The Community Bill of Rights Ordinance is the vehicle for the exercise of that right – declaring that "all government ought to be instituted and supported for the security and protection of the community as such. . .[and that] all power is inherent in the people, and all free governments are founded on their authority and instituted for their peace, safety, and happiness." [Doc. 1-1 (Ordinance at ¶¶ 5-6) (*quoting* the 1776 PENNSYLVANIA CONSTITUTION and PA. CONST. Art.1, §2)].

The people of Grant Township then asserted their right to local, community self-government to secure and protect their civil, political, and environmental rights by creating a local bill of rights, which protects their rights to clean air, water, and soil; to scenic preservation; to environmental rights; and to a sustainable energy future. They then prohibited those activities which would violate those rights, including the commercial deposition of oil and gas wastes within the Township.[60] [Doc. 1-1 (Ordinance at § 3(a))].

Finally, the people of Grant Township moved to locally eliminate those doctrines which would traditionally prevent them from securing and protecting their rights. Accordingly, they included the following provision in the Ordinance:

> Corporations that violate this Ordinance, or that seek to violate this Ordinance, shall not be deemed to be "persons," nor possess any other legal rights, privileges, powers, or protections which would interfere with the rights or prohibitions enumerated by this Ordinance. "Rights, privileges, powers, or protections" shall include the power to assert state or federal preemptive laws in an attempt to overturn this Ordinance, and the power to assert that the people of the municipality lack the authority to adopt this Ordinance.

[Doc. 1-1 (Ordinance at §5(a)].

The people's constitutional right to local, community self-government guarantees their authority to adopt their local bill of rights, their authority to prohibit activities that would violate that local bill of rights, and their authority to adopt provisions which protect their bill of rights from competing legal doctrines which would otherwise allow both private corporations and the state government to nullify that bill of rights.

From the perspective of the people of Grant Township, this case is about forcing this Court to pick a side – to either vindicate the people's right to local, community self-government over the "rights" claimed by a private corporation, or to again elevate the right of a private corporation over the heads of the very people that this constitutional system was ostensibly designed to protect.

Precisely because the right of the people of Grant to local, community self-government requires this Court to choose the former, rather than the latter, the Defendant is entitled to judgment on the pleadings.

> **V.   The Defendant is entitled to judgment on the pleadings because it has an obligation as a trustee under Article I, §27 of the Pennsylvania Constitution, and it has satisfied its obligations by adopting the Ordinance.**

The Pennsylvania Constitution, at Article I, §27, establishes that

The people have a right to clean air, pure water, and to the preservation of the natural, scenic, historic, and esthetic values of the environment. Pennsylvania's public natural resources are the common property of all the people, including generations yet to come. As trustee of these resources, the Commonwealth shall conserve and maintain them for the benefit of all the people.
PA CONST. Art. 1, §27.

In Robinson Township et al. v. Commonwealth of Pennsylvania, et al., the Pennsylvania Supreme Court examined whether Act 13 of 2012 (which, among other provisions, prohibited local regulation of oil and gas operations and overrode certain locally adopted zoning provisions dealing with oil and gas extraction), violated the environmental guarantees of Article I, §27 of the Pennsylvania Constitution. *Robinson Township et al. v. Commonwealth of Pennsylvania*, 83 A.3d 901 (Pa. 2013).[61] In examining the reach of §27, the Court explained that it contained two separate guarantees – the first establishing citizens' environmental rights, and the second establishing governments within the Commonwealth as trustees for the protection of natural resources. *Id.* at 950-952. The Court then recognized that the "constitutional obligation binds all government, state or local, concurrently." *Id.* at 952.

In examining the responsibility of local governments as trustees for natural resources of the Commonwealth, the Court explained that

The Commonwealth is a named trustee and, notably, duties and powers attendant to the trust are not vested exclusively in any single branch of Pennsylvania's government. The plain intent of the provision is to permit the checks and balances of government to operate in their usual fashion for the benefit of the people in order to accomplish the purposes of the trust. This includes local government. . . . The explicit terms of the trust require the government to 'conserve and maintain' the corpus of the trust. . . [which] implicates a duty to prevent and remedy the degradation, diminution, or depletion of our public natural resources.

The second obligation peculiar to the trustee is, as the Commonwealth recognizes, to act affirmatively to protect the environment, via legislative action. . . With the public trust paradigm of Section 27, the beneficiaries of the trust are "all the people" of Pennsylvania, including generations yet to come. The trust's beneficiary designation has two obvious implications: first, the trustee has an obligation to deal impartially with all beneficiaries, and, second, the trustee has an obligation to balance the interests of present and future beneficiaries.

Id. at 959 (citations omitted).

In striking parts of the Oil and Gas Act as those provisions related to overriding the authority of local governments to regulate oil and gas operations, the Court declared that

development of the natural gas industry in the Commonwealth unquestionably has and will have a lasting, and undeniably detrimental, impact on the quality of these corporate aspects of Pennsylvania's environment, which are part of the public trust. . . By any responsible account, the exploitation of the Marcellus Shale Formation will produce a detrimental effect on the environment, on the people, their children, and future generations, and potentially on the public purse, perhaps rivaling the environmental effects of coal extraction. . . Contrary to the Commonwealth's characterization of the dispute, the citizens seek not to expand the authority of local government but to vindicate fundamental constitutional rights that, they say, have been compromised. . . Act 13 thus commands municipalities to ignore their obligations under Article I, Section 27 and further directs municipalities to take affirmative actions to undo existing protections of the environmental in their localities. . . it is apparent that the Article I, Section 27 constitutional commands have been swept aside.

Id. at 976 (citations omitted).

In the instant case, not only have the residents of the community secured their environmental rights through local legislation – which recognizes and protects many of the same rights which are explicitly protected by Article I, Section 27[62] – the Township has also carried out its trustee obligations by banning commercial deposition as a violation of those rights. In support of that lawmaking, the Community Bill of Rights Ordinance specifically finds that

> the depositing of waste from oil and gas extraction is economically and environmentally unsustainable, in that it damages property values and the natural environment, and places the health of residents at risk, while failing to provide real benefits to the people of this community.

[Doc. 1-1 (Ordinance at ¶ 1).

Thus, not only have the residents of the community acted to secure and protect their rights under the Pennsylvania Constitution, they have worked with their Township officials to carry out its role as constitutional trustee of the Commonwealth's natural resources. Because the Township has acted in accordance with, and under the guidance of, those constitutional guarantees and requirements, the Defendant is entitled to judgment on the pleadings.

VI.   Conclusion.

For the reasons asserted herein, the Defendant is entitled to judgment on the pleadings, the dismissal of the instant action, and a declaration that the Plaintiff is liable for seeking to violate the right of the people of Grant Township to local, community self-government.

Respectfully submitted this *15th* Day of **December,** 2014.

For Defendant Grant Township:

/s *Thomas Alan Linzey*
Thomas Alan Linzey, Esq.
Community Environmental Legal Defense Fund
P.O. Box 360
Mercersburg, Pennsylvania 17236
(717) 498-0054 (v)

[1] The Ordinance declares that "this community finds that the depositing of waste from oil and gas extraction is economically and environmentally unsustainable, in that it damages property values and the natural environment, and places the health of residents at risk, while failing to provide real benefits to the people of this community." [Doc. 1-1 (Ordinance at ¶1)]. *See infra*, note 60.

[2] This section of the brief contains a lengthy historical discussion atypical of most court filings. Such a discussion, however, is necessary for an understanding of the origins of the fundamental and unalienable right of local, community self-government upon which the Ordinance is based. The Defendant also understands that arguments in later sections of the brief raise issues related to what may be considered "well-settled" law. Courts in this country, of course, have a history of revisiting that law. *See, e.g., Brown v. Board of Education*, 347 U.S. 483, 74 S.Ct. 686 (1954) (overruling *Plessy v. Ferguson*, 163 U.S. 537, 16 S.Ct. 1138 (1896)); *Whitewood v. Wolf*, 992 F. Supp. 2d 410 (M.D.PA 2014) (rejecting *Baker v. Nelson* as binding precedent, 291 Minn. 310, 191 N.W.2d 185 (1971)), *dismissed based on want of a substantial federal question*, 409 U.S. 810 (1972); *see also McDonald v. City of Chicago, Ill.*, 561 U.S. 742, 130 S.Ct. 3020 (2010) (delineating a lengthy history of overruled precedent).

[3] McQuillan, A TREATISE ON THE LAW OF MUNICIPAL CORPORATIONS, Vol. 1 at 152 (1911) ("in this country from the beginning, political power has been exercised by citizens of the various local communities as local communities, and this constitutes the most important feature in our system of government.").

[4] The Mayflower Compact at ¶ 2 (http://en.wikipedia.org/wiki/Mayflower_Compact) (accessed November 10, 2014).

[5] *See* the Avalon Project at Yale Law School, Fundamental Orders of 1639 (http://avalon.law.yale.edu/17th_century/order.asp) (accessed November 8, 2014).

[6] *See* the Avalon Project at Yale Law School, the Articles of Confederation of the United Colonies of New England, May 19, 1643 (http://avalon.law.yale.edu/17th_century/art1613.asp) (accessed November 8, 2014). Others proceeding to create self-governing jurisdictions included the Popham Colony in present-day Maine, the Saybrook Colony of present-day Connecticut, and the colonies of New Haven, New Netherland, East Jersey, West Jersey, and the Province of Carolina, among many others.

[7] An English writer in the middle of the nineteenth century explained how the freedom of a society correlates with the strength of local government: "There are two elements to which every form of Government may be reduced. These are LOCAL SELF-GOVERNMENT on the one hand, and CENTRALIZATION on the other. According as the former or the latter of these exists more or less predominant, will the state of any nation be the more or less free, happy, progressive, truly prosperous, and safe.... LOCAL SELF-GOVERNMENT is that system of Government under which the greatest number of minds, knowing the most, and having the fullest opportunities of knowing it, about the special matter in hand, and having the greatest interest in its well-working, have the management of it, or control over it. CENTRALIZATION is that system of Government under which the smallest number of minds, and those knowing the least, and having the fewest opportunities of knowing it, about the special matter in hand, and having the smallest interest in its well-working, have the management of it, or control over it." Smith, Joshua Toulmin, LOCAL SELF-GOVERNMENT AND CENTRALIZATION 11, 12 (1851).

[8] Foreshadowing the American Revolutionary War, there were no fewer than a dozen armed peoples' revolts against British rule between 1676 and the 1760's. As with the Revolutionary War, almost all were triggered by British efforts to strip the colonists of self-governing authority. They included Bacon's Rebellion of 1676 (driven by the royal governor's refusal to implement measures adopted by the Virginia legislature); Culpeper's Rebellion of 1677 (evicting the proprietary government of Carolina due to the collection of a British-imposed tobacco duty); the Boston Revolt of 1689 (imprisoning the royal governor and re-establishing an earlier form of representative government); and the Mast Tree Riot of 1734 (against the royal government's prohibition on colonial use of mature pine trees used by the English navy for masts). Miller, ORIGINS OF THE AMERICAN REVOLUTION 38 (1962).

[9] The Boston Town Meeting was a regular event to which all of the people of Boston were invited to discuss, and vote upon, issues important to Bostonians. The Town Meeting form of government, unique to New England, continues today. All New England Towns hold an annual Town Meeting (and special Town Meetings in between) to vote on resolutions and laws proposed by residents. Current Massachusetts law recognizing the form and structure of those Town Meetings can be found at Chapter 43-A of the General Laws of the Commonwealth of Massachusetts.

[10]The Acts included the Quebec Act (stripping the people of Quebec of most governing authority, it was seen as a parliamentary model for future treatment of the colonists); the Administration of Justice Act (requiring trials of certain British officers to occur in British courts, removing the jurisdiction of colonial courts over them); the Massachusetts Government Act (banning Town Meetings without the consent of the royal Governor, and canceling part of the Colony's original Charter by eliminating the authority of the colonial assembly to elect the Executive Council); and the Quartering Act (requiring the colonies to provide housing for British soldiers over the refusal of the assemblies of several states to do so).

[11] The 1691 Charter for the Massachusetts Bay Colony provided that all residents of the Colony "shall have and enjoy all liberties and immunities of free and natural subjects. . . as if they and every one of them were born within this our realm of England." Beach, SAMUEL ADAMS: THE FATEFUL YEARS 1764-1776 48 (1965).

[12] The Avalon Project at Yale Law School, THE MECKLENBURGH RESOLUTIONS (May 20, 1775) (http://avalon.law.yale.edu/18th_century/nc06.asp) (accessed November 9, 2014).

[13] *Id.* at Virginia Declaration of Rights (http://avalon.law.yale.edu/18th_century/virginia.asp) (accessed November 10, 2014) (emphasis added).

[14] The great majority of the numerous facts "submitted to a candid world" by the Declaration to document the colonists' grievances with the crown concerned the power of self-government, beginning with the very first: "He has refused his Assent to Laws the most wholesome and necessary for the public good."

[15] DECL. OF INDEPENDENCE at ¶ 2 ("That all men. . . are endowed by their Creator with certain unalienable rights; that among these are life, liberty, and the pursuit of happiness.").

[16] *Id.* ("that, to secure these rights, governments are instituted among men.").

[17] *Id.* ("deriving their just powers from the consent of the governed.").

[18] *Id.* ("whenever any form of government becomes destructive of these ends, it is the right of the people to alter or to abolish it, and to institute new government, laying its foundation on such principles, and organizing its powers in such form, as to them shall seem most likely to effect their

safety and happiness. . . it is their right, it is their duty, to throw off such government.").

[19]The people of two states, New York and Connecticut, adopted the text of the Declaration directly into their state constitutions; the people of eight states adopted a Declaration of Rights that restated the four principles of the Declaration; and the people of four states—New Jersey, Georgia, South Carolina, and New Hampshire—included the principles of the Declaration in the text of the preamble to their state constitutions. *See* The Avalon Project at Yale Law School at Constitution of New York (April 20, 1777); Constitution of New Jersey (July 2, 1776); Constitution of Georgia (February 5, 1777); Constitution of South Carolina (March 26, 1776); Constitution of New Hampshire (January 5, 1776); Constitution of Delaware (September 21, 1776); Constitution of Maryland (November 11, 1776), Constitution of North Carolina (December 18, 1776); Constitution of Pennsylvania (September 28, 1776); Constitution of Virginia (June 29, 1776); Constitution of Vermont (July 8, 1777), http://avalon.law.yale.edu/subject_menus/18th.asp (accessed November 11, 2014).

[20] *See* The Avalon Project at Yale Law School, Constitution of Pennsylvania at ¶¶ 2-5 (September 28, 1776) (http://avalon.law.yale.edu/18th_century/pa08.asp) (accessed November 9, 2014) (emphasis added); Gormley, THE PENNSYLVANIA CONSTITUTION at 43–44 (the Pennsylvania Constitution "explicitly incorporated the Declaration of Rights into the Constitution with the mandate that it 'ought never to be violated on any pretence whatever.'").

[21] The Avalon Project at Yale Law School, Constitution of Pennsylvania at ¶5 (September 28, 1776) (http://avalon.law.yale.edu/18th_century/pa08.asp) (accessed August 8, 2014) (emphasis added). In his treatise on the Pennsylvania Constitution, Ken Gormley writes, "[m]any modern-day lawyers are surprised to learn that Pennsylvania's Constitution of 1776 was widely viewed as the most radically democratic of all the early state constitutions." Gormley, THE PENNSYLVANIA CONSTITUTION 3 (2004).

[22] *See* John L. Gedid and Ken Gormley, *et al.*, THE PENNSYLVANIA CONSTITUTION, 37-41 (2004) (describing how disenfranchised communities in the western part of the state fought to exercise political power with communities around Philadelphia); Maier, AMERICAN SCRIPTURE, ch. 2 (1997) (describing how Pennsylvania's legislative assembly that resisted separation from Great Britain dissolved and a

constitutional convention composed of members favoring self-governance formed); Bockelman, Wayne L., LOCAL GOVERNMENT IN COLONIAL PENNSYLVANIA 9-14 (1969).

[23] *See* PENNSYLVANIA CONSTITUTION OF 1790, Art. IX Declaration of Rights, sec. XXVI (reprinted in Gormley, THE PENNSYLVANIA CONSTITUTION at 883); Gormley, THE PENNSYLVANIA CONSTITUTION at 56 ("the bad experience with legislative incursions on individual rights under the 1776 Pennsylvania Constitution led to express exception from legislative power of rights contained in the Declaration of Rights of the Constitution of 1790.").

[24] According to John L. Gedid, "[t]he Whigs also believed that individuals inherently possessed natural rights, and that these rights did not have to be created by positive law or statute. This natural right theory meant that rights existed even if the legislature had not recognized them and that even the legislature could not take away these inherent natural rights." Gormley, THE PENNSYLVANIA CONSTITUTION at 40.

[25] As one writer said, "The people, who are sovereigns of the state, possess a power to alter when and in what way they please. To say [otherwise] ... is to make the thing created, greater than the power that created it." Fed. Gazette, 18 Mar. 1789 (reprinted in Matthew J. Herrington, *Popular Sovereignty in Pennsylvania 1776–1791*, 67 TEMP. L. REV. 575 (1994)).

[26] This debate was forced by the people of the states through their ratifying conventions. The conventions of many states chose to use the ratification process as another vehicle for securing their right to community self-government. They did so by offering amendments that incorporated the principles of the Declaration directly into the text of the Constitution. The people who voted to reject the Constitution outright (and the populations they represented), and the people who refused to ratify without the offering of those local self-government amendments (and the populations they represented) constituted a majority of the people living within the United States at the time of ratification. *See* The Avalon Project at Yale Law School at Ratification of the Constitution by the Various States (http://avalon.law.yale.edu/subject_menus/18th.asp) (accessed November 11, 2014).

Mirroring the Declaration of Rights already adopted by a majority of people within a majority of states in their own constitutions, the people of Virginia ratified the Constitution subject to the following amendments:

1st. That there are certain natural rights of which men when they form a social compact cannot deprive or divest their posterity, among which are the enjoyment of life, and liberty, with the means of acquiring, possessing and protecting property, and pursuing and obtaining happiness and safety.

2d. That all power is naturally vested in, and consequently derived from, the people; that magistrates therefore are their trustees, and agents, and at all times amenable to them.

3d. That the Government ought to be instituted for the common benefit, protection and security of the people; and that the doctrine of non-resistance against arbitrary power and oppression, is absurd, slavish, and destructive to the good and happiness of mankind.

The Avalon Project at Yale Law School, RATIFICATION OF THE CONSTITUTION BY THE STATE OF VIRGINIA (June 26, 1788) (http://avalon.law.yale.edu/18th_century/ratva.asp) (accessed November 8, 2014).

[27]Madison proposed amending the Constitution's preamble to include the following language:

> "That all power is originally vested in, and consequently derived from the people.

> That government is instituted, and ought to be exercised for the benefit of the people, which consists in the enjoyment of life and liberty, with the right of acquiring and using property, and generally of pursuing and obtaining happiness and safety.

> That the people have an indubitable, unalienable, and indefeasible right to reform or change their government, whenever it be found adverse or inadequate to the purposes of its institution."

U.S. House of Representatives, June 8, 1789

(http://teachingamericanhistory.org/bor/madison_17890608/) (accessed November 8, 2014).

[28] U.S. House of Representatives, August 14, 1789 (www.teachingamericanhistory.org/bor/select-committee-report/) (accessed November 8, 2014).

[29] Speaking at the Pennsylvania convention that ratified the federal Constitution, James Wilson said: "His [Mr. Findley's] position is, that the supreme power resides in the States, as governments; and mine is, that it resides in the people, as the fountain of government; that the people have not—that the people mean not—and that the people ought not, to part with it to any government whatsoever. They can delegate it in such proportions, to such bodies, on such terms, and under such limitations, as they think proper." James Wilson, Pennsylvania Ratifying Convention, 4 Dec. 1787 (reprinted in Philip B. Kurland, THE FOUNDERS' CONSTITUTION VOLUME ONE at 62).

[30] The U.S. Constitution also secures the right to local, community self-government at Article IV, §4: "The United States shall guarantee to every State in this Union a Republican Form of Government."

[31] Preemption, when exercised to set a ceiling, rather than a floor, for local lawmaking in protection of rights, inherently violates the right to local, community self-government. That doctrine, when exercised in that way, is the focus of the preemption section of this Brief. The people of Grant seek to expand their civil, political, and environmental rights at the municipal level in much the same way that States have expanded certain rights beyond those explicitly guaranteed by the federal bill of rights. *See* William J. Brennan, Jr., *State Constitutions and the Protection of Individual Rights*, 90 HARV. L.REV. 489 (1977).

[32] As will be seen in later sections of this Brief, because corporate "rights" are rooted in the federal constitution, corporations routinely exercise those "rights" to overturn not only local laws, but also state and federal ones.

[33] *See, e.g.*, the American Declaration of Independence, ¶1 *et seq.* (U.S. 1776) (listing the grievances of the colonists).

[34] James K. Hosmer, SAMUEL ADAMS 212 (1885) (stating that the British Parliament hoped that "the prosperity of the East India Company would be furthered, which for some time past, owing to the colonial non-importation agreements, had been obliged to see its tea accumulate in its warehouses, until the amount reached 17,000,000 pounds").

[35] *See Louis K. Liggett Co., v. Lee*, 288 U.S. 517 (1933) (Brandeis, J., dissenting) (stating that "at first the corporate privilege was granted sparingly; and only when the grant seemed necessary in order to procure for the community some specific benefit otherwise unattainable." Here, too, Brandeis answered the question of why incorporation for business was commonly denied long after it had been freely granted for religious,

educational, and charitable purposes: "It was denied because of fear. Fear of encroachment upon the liberties and opportunities of the individual. Fear of the subjection of labor to capital. Fear of monopoly. Fear that absorption of capital by corporations, and their perpetual life, might bring evils similar to those which attended mortmain. There was a sense of some insidious menace inherent in large aggregations of capital, particularly when held by corporations.").

[36] Robert Hamilton, THE LAW OF CORPORATIONS 6 (1991). As the Supreme Court of Virginia reasoned in 1809, if the applicant's "object is merely private or selfish; if it is detrimental to, or not promotive of, the public good, they have no adequate claim upon the legislature for the privileges." Morton J. Horwitz, THE TRANSFORMATION OF AMERICAN LAW, 1780-1860 112 (1977).

[37] *See St. Louis, I.M. & S Ry. Co. v. Paul*, 173 U.S. 404 (1899) (declaring that corporations are "creations of state"); *Bank of Augusta v. Earle*, 38 U.S. 519, 520 (1839) (stating that "corporations are municipal creations of states"); *United States v. Morton Salt Co.*, 338 U.S. 632, 650 (1950) (explaining that corporations "are endowed with public attributes. They have a collective impact upon society, from which they derive the privilege as artificial entities"); *Hale v. Henkel*, 201 U.S. 43, 75 (1906) (declaring that "the corporation is a creature of the state. It is presumed to be incorporated for the benefit of the public. . . . Its rights to act as a corporation are only preserved to it so long as it obeys the laws of its creation"); *Chincleclamouche Lumber & Broom Co. v. Commonwealth*, 100 Pa. 438, 444 (Pa. 1881) (stating that "the objects for which a corporation is created are universally such as the government wishes to promote. They are deemed beneficial to the country"); *See also, People v. North River Sugar Refining Company*, 24 N.E. 834, 835 (NY 1890) (declaring that "[t]he life of a corporation is, indeed, less than that of the humblest citizen."); *F.E. Nugent Funeral Home v. Beamish*, 173 A. 177, 179 (Pa. 1934) (declaring that "[c]orporations organized under a state's laws. . . depend on it alone for power and authority"); *People v. Curtice*, 117 P. 357, 360 (Colo. 1911) (declaring that "[i]t is in no sense a sovereign corporation, because it rests on the will of the people of the entire state and continues only so long as the people of the entire state desire it to continue").

[38] *See, e.g., Virginia Bankshares v. Sandberg*, 501 U.S. 1083, 1093 (1991); *Kamen v. Kember Fin. Servs.*, 500 U.S. 90, 99 (1991); *Braswell v. United States*, 487 U.S. 99, 105 (1988); *Burks v. Lasker*, 441 U.S. 471, 478 (1979) (declaring that "corporations are creatures of state law [] and it is state law which is the font of corporate directors' powers"); *First Nat'l Bank of Boston v. Bellotti*, 435 U.S. 765 (1978); *Santa Fe Industries, Inc. v. Green*, 430

U.S. 462, 479 (1977); *Cort v. Ash*, 422 U.S. 66, 84 (1975); *United Steelworkers of America v. R.H. Bouligny, Inc.*, 382 U.S. 145, 147 (1965); *Shapiro v. United States*, 335 U.S. 1, 66 (1948); *Ferry v. Ramsey*, 277 U.S. 88, 96-97 (1928); *Essgee Co. of China v. United States*, 262 U.S. 151, 155 (1923); *Yazoo & M.V.R.Co. v. Clarksdale*, 257 U.S. 10, 26 (1921); *United States v. American Tobacco Co.*, 221 U.S. 106, 142-143 (1911); *Wilson v. United States*, 221 U.S. 361, 383 (1911); *Hale v. Henkel*, 201 U.S. 43 (1906); *Terre Haute & I.R.Co. v. Indiana*, 194 U.S. 579, 584 (1904); *Fidelity Mut. Life Asso. v. Mettler*, 185 U.S. 308 327 (1902); *Hancock Mut. Life Ins. Co. v. Warren*, 181 U.S. 73, 76 (1901); *Jellenik v. Huron Copper Mining Co.*, 177 U.S. 1, 11-13 (1900); *Woodruff v. Mississippi*, 162 U.S. 291, 299, 309 (1896); *Philadelphia & Southern Mail S.S. Co. v. Pennsylvania*, 122 U.S. 326 (1887); *Sinking-Fund Cases*, 99 U.S. 700, 718 (1878); *Railroad Co. v. Maryland*, 88 U.S. 456, 469, 471 (1874); *Dodge v. Woolsey*, 59 U.S. 331 (1855); *Bank of Augusta v. Earle*, 38 U.S. 519, 520 (1839); *Briscoe v. President & Directors of Bank of Kentucky*, 36 U.S. 257, 328 (1837).

[39] As a general principal of justice, rights have long been understood to accrue to the living, and not to the dead, nor to inanimate matter. Thomas Paine's *Common Sense* (1776), credited with inspiring the popular call for American independence, argued that hereditary government and the rule of the dead over the living—expressed as oppressive legal precedent—defined the "old form" of government, while deference to the rights of the living characterized the new. *See also* Thomas Jefferson, who asked:

> Can one generation bind another, and all others, in succession forever? I think not. The Creator made the earth for the living, not the dead. Rights and powers can belong only to persons, not to things, not to mere matter unendowed with will. The dead are not even things...To what then are attached the rights and powers they held while in the form of men? A generation may bind itself as long as its majority continues in life; when that has disappeared, another majority is in its place, holding all the rights and powers their predecessors once held, and may change their laws and institutions to suit themselves. Nothing then is unchangeable but the inherent and inalienable rights of man!

Thomas Jefferson, *Letter to Major John Cartwright*, (June 5, 1824).

[40] Corporations were declared to be "persons" entitled to Fourteenth Amendment protections in *Santa Clara County v. Southern Pacific Railroad Company*, 118 U.S. 394 (1886) and *Minneapolis & St. Louis Railroad Company v. Beckwith*, 129 U.S. 26 (1889).

[41] Corporations were declared to be entitled to First Amendment protections in *First National Bank of Boston v. Bellotti*, 435 U.S. 765 (1978); to Fourth Amendment protections in *Hale v. Henkel*, 201 U.S. 43 (1906); and to Fifth Amendment protections in *Noble v. Union River Logging R. Co.*, 147 U.S. 165 (1893); *Pennsylvania Coal Co. v. Mahon*, 260 U.S. 393 (1922); and *Fong Foo v. United States*, 369 U.S. 141 (1962). Corporations have been discovered in other Amendments, including the Seventh Amendment, but this Brief focuses solely on those Amendments relevant to the instant suit.

[42] Courts conferred Contracts Clause protections on corporate charters in *Dartmouth College v. Woodward*, 4 Wheat. 518 (1816). For a contemporary use of the Contracts Clause to override local decisionmaking, *see City of New Orleans v. Bellsouth Telecommunications, Inc.* 690 F.3d 312 (5th Cir. 2012) (striking a law that imposed new consideration on a telecommunications corporation for the use of rights-of-way within the City). For an example of Commerce Clause protections for corporations, see, for example, *South Dakota Farm Bureau, Inc. et al. v. Hazeltine*, 340 F.3d 583 (8th Cir. 2003) (striking down the State's anti-corporate farming law as violating agribusiness corporations' rights under the Commerce Clause).

[43] Morton J. Horwitz, THE TRANSFORMATION OF AMERICAN LAW 1870-1960 101 (1992) (explaining that "[t]he efforts by legal thinkers to legitimate the business corporation during the 1890's were buttressed by a stunning reversal in American economic thought – a movement to defend and justify as inevitable the emergence of large-scale corporate concentration"). *Id.* at 80, 145.

[44] *See Connecticut General Life Insurance Co. v. Johnson*, 303 U.S. 77, 85-90 (1938) (Black, J., dissenting) (declaring that "[n]either the history nor the language of the Fourteenth Amendment justifies the belief that corporations are included within its protection"); *Wheeling Steel Corp. v. Glander*, 337 U.S. 562, 576-581 (1949) (Douglas, J., and Black, J., dissenting) (declaring that "I can only conclude that the *Santa Clara* case was wrong and should be overruled"); *See also, Hale v. Henkel*, 201 U.S. 43, 78 (1906) (Harlan, J., concurring) (declaring that "in my opinion, a corporation—an artificial being, invisible, intangible, and existing only in contemplation of law—cannot claim the immunity given by the 4th Amendment; for it is not a part of the 'people' within the meaning of that Amendment. Nor is it embraced by the word "persons" in the Amendment"); *Bell v. Maryland*, 378 U.S. 226, 263 (1964) (Douglas, J., dissenting) (declaring that "[t]he revolutionary change effected by affirmance in these sit-in cases would be much more damaging to an open and free society than what the Court did when it gave the corporation the sword and shield of the Due Process and Equal Protection Clauses of the

Fourteenth Amendment"); *First National Bank of Boston v. Bellotti*, 435 U.S. 765, 822 (1978) (Rehnquist, J., dissenting) (declaring that "[t]his Court decided at an early date, with neither argument nor discussion, that a business corporation is a 'person' entitled to the protection of the Equal Protection Clause of the Fourteenth Amendment"); *Citizens United v. Federal Election Commission*, 558 U.S. 310, 466 (2010) (Stevens, J., concurring in part, dissenting in part) ("corporations have no consciences, no beliefs, no feelings, no thoughts, no desires. . . they are not themselves members of "We the People" by whom and for whom our Constitution was established. . . [today's decision] is thus a rejection of the common sense of the American people, who have recognized a need to prevent corporations from undermining self-government since the founding. . ."); *Burwell v. Hobby Lobby Stores, Inc.*, 134 S.Ct. 2751, 2802 (2014) (Ginsburg, J., dissenting) (the "exercise of religion is characteristic of natural persons, not artificial legal entities.").

[45] In 2010, the Supreme Court invalidated federal campaign finance laws as violative of the corporate "right" to free speech as a "person." *Citizens United v. Federal Election Commission*, 558 U.S. 50 (2010); *See International Dairy Foods v. Amestoy*, 92 F.3d 67 (2nd Cir. 1996) (nullifying a dairy labeling law in Vermont that violated the corporate "right" not to be compelled to speak under the First Amendment); *CTLA-The Wireless Association v. City and County of San Francisco*, No. 11-17707, No. 11-17773 (9th Cir., unreported memorandum opinion, Sep. 10, 2012) (striking a City law requiring retail point-of-purchase warnings for health risks from cellular telephone radio emissions as a violation of speech rights); *First National Bank of Boston v. Bellotti*, 435 U.S. 765 (1978) (nullifying a state law banning corporate spending on political referenda); *Pacific Gas & Elec. Co. v. Public Utilities Comm'n*, 475 U.S. 1 (1986) (preventing utility ratepayers from using space within a utility's monthly billing envelopes for consumer communications); *Central Hudson Gas & Electric Corp. v. Public Utilities Comm'n*, 447 U.S. 557 (1980) (overturning regulations aimed at conserving electricity during the 1970's energy crisis); *Jacobus v. State of Alaska*, 338 F.3d 1095 (9th Cir. 2003) (banning states from curtailing corporate participation in electoral activities as a violation of free speech rights).

[46] *Pennsylvania Coal Co. v. Mahon*, 260 U.S. 393 (1922) (overturning a Pennsylvania law - the Kohler Act – which required coal operators to leave pillars of coal in place to prevent subsidence, as violating the Fifth Amendment rights of coal corporations).

[47] *See Dartmouth College v. Woodward*, 4 Wheat. 518 (1816) (declaring that corporate charters were contracts protected by the Constitution's Contracts Clause, and therefore, that state legislatures were prohibited

from unilaterally altering those charters. Interestingly, the Court also explained that municipal charters were not subject to the same prohibitions, thus enabling States to alter laws governing municipal corporations at will).

[48] *South Dakota Farm Bureau, Inc. et al., v. Hazeltine*, 340 F.3d 583 (8th Cir. 2003) (using the Commerce Clause to overturn South Dakota's anti-corporate farming law, which banned corporations from owning farmland or engaging in farming within the State); *See Smithfield Foods, Inc. v. Miller*, 367 F.3d 1061 (8th Cir. 2003) (striking down laws regulating corporate involvement in hog production); *Synagro-WWT, Inc. v. Rush Township*, 204 F. Supp. 2d 827 (M.D. Pa. 2002), 299 F. Supp. 2d 410 (M.D. Pa. 2003) (striking down laws intended to protect residents from corporate-hauled land applied sewage sludge); *H. P. Hood & Sons, Inc. v. Du Mond*, 336 U.S. 525 (1949) (striking down laws dealing with milk licenses intended to protect competition and milk supply); *Baldwin v. G.A.F. Seelig, Inc.*, 294 U.S. 511 (1935) (striking down laws mandating milk dealer prices which were adopted to ensure economically viable dairy farming).

[49] In her opinion, Judge O'Dell Seneca held that corporations' privacy interests were not protected by the Pennsylvania Constitution's Declaration of Rights.

[50] *See Chemical Waste Management, Inc. v. Hunt*, 504 U.S. 334 (1992).

[51] *See, e.g.,* "Charter of King Charles II of England to William Penn," 4 March 1681, section V, which allowed Pennsylvania the power to make laws for the good and happy government of the colony, "Provided; Nevertheless, that the said Lawes bee consonant to reason, and bee not repugnant or contrarie, but as neere as conveniently may bee agreeable to the Lawes, statutes and rights of this our Kingdome of England…"

[52] Joshua Smith wrote in his English treatise: "The practical idea, and the result, of Centralization … is … that the State is something apart from its members; and that it has the function, and the right, to keep each and all of those members within a certain tether, the length of which it belongs to it to determine, and on which no right nor responsibility of judging belongs to them." Smith, Joshua Toulmin, LOCAL SELF-GOVERNMENT AND CENTRALIZATION 34 (1851).

[53] In his English treatise, Joshua Smith showed how the right of self-government is inextricably bound to a duty, the marriage of which constitutes freedom: "Not by having our affairs well managed *for* us, by others, are we, or can we ever be, free, or maintain free Institutions; but by having the ever-present consciousness that it is to us ourselves that the

right and the responsibility belong of doing, and doing well, what the common welfare, or our own, demands." Smith, Joshua Toulmin, LOCAL SELF-GOVERNMENT AND CENTRALIZATION, 33–34 (1851).

[54] Dillon's Rule only applies to the specific relationship between municipal corporations and the State. Here, the people of Grant Township adopted the Ordinance directly, in tandem with Grant Township. Thus, the Ordinance establishes that "We the People of Grant Township hereby adopt this Community Bill of Rights Ordinance." [Doc. 1-1 (Ordinance at ¶ 8)]. The Ordinance also specifically establishes that the "use of the municipal corporation 'Grant Township' by the people for the making and enforcement of this law shall not be deemed, by any authority, to eliminate, limit, or reduce that sovereign right" to local self-government. [Doc. 1-1 (Ordinance at §2(a))].

[55] At a time when centralization in England was encroaching on local government, Joshua Smith wrote this about the very authority to form local governments, specifically with charters for boroughs: "They are founded, altogether, on the fundamental ideas of Local Self-Government which run through the whole spirit and practice of the Constitution. If, in any place, the inhabitants agree together to have that special form of united existence which is called a borough, it is their own affair; and, at the Common Law, it is their inherent right so to agree. Having thus agreed, they simply go to the Crown, as the head ministerial officer, and claim, as of common right, that it shall endorse their agreement, so as to make it a matter of permanent record. It is purely in its ministerial capacity that the Crown has anything to do with such charters. The agreement of the inhabitants is their sole legal ground and support.... The Crown has, legally, no discretion in the matter...." Smith, Joshua Toulmin, LOCAL SELF-GOVERNMENT AND CENTRALIZATION 101 (1851).

[56] As Eugene McQuillan wrote: "Therefore, it appears clear that in a government in which the legislative power of the state is not omnipotent, and in which it is axiomatic that local self-government is not a mere privilege, but a matter of absolute political right, the existence of unlimited authority in the law making body to concentrate all the powers of local government in the state does not exist." McQuillan, A TREATISE ON THE LAW OF MUNICIPAL CORPORATIONS 385 (1911).

[57]As with the application of Dillon's Rule to Grant Township's adoption of the Community Bill of Rights Ordinance, preemption doctrine specifically applies only to the relationship between the State and municipal corporations. Here, the people of Grant Township adopted the

Ordinance directly, in tandem with Grant Township. Thus, the Ordinance establishes that "We the People of Grant Township hereby adopt this Community Bill of Rights Ordinance." [Doc. 1-1 (Ordinance at ¶ 8)]. The Ordinance also specifically establishes that the "use of the municipal corporation 'Grant Township' by the people for the making and enforcement of this law shall not be deemed, by any authority, to eliminate, limit, or reduce that sovereign right" to local self-government. [Doc. 1-1 (Ordinance at §2(a))]. While that may carve out an exception to the application of preemption principles for laws adopted directly by the people of a locality, the doctrine of preemption cannot, in the end, co-exist with the right of the people to local, community self-government when the relevant state law seeks to establish a ceiling, rather than a floor, for local rights-based lawmaking.

[58]Laws resulting from the priorities of those corporations have preempted local control over issues including **liquor** (47 P.S. §1-101 *et seq.*; *see Petition of Hilovsky*, 379 Pa. 118, 108 A.2d 705 (1954) (striking a local ordinance that regulated service of liquor in restaurants)); **mining** (52 P.S. §681.1 *et seq.* (Act of June 27, 1947); *see Harris-Walsh, Inc. v. Borough of Dickson City*, 216 A.2d 329 (Pa.1966) (striking a local ordinance regulating anthracite coal mining within the municipality)); *see also*, 53 P.S. §10603(i) (amending the Municipalities Planning Code to mandate that each municipality allow "reasonable development of minerals")); **banking** (7 P.S. § 101 *et. seq.*; *see City of Pittsburgh v. Allegheny Valley Bank of Pittsburgh*, 488 Pa. 544, 412 A.2d 1366 (1980) (striking a local tax on banks)); **oil and gas wells** (Oil and Gas Act, 58 P.S. § 601.602; *see Range Resources Appalachia v. Salem Twp.*, 964 A.2d 869 (Pa. 2009) (striking a township's oil and gas regulatory scheme, in part because it was more stringent that state regulation)); **factory farming** (Right to Farm Act amendment, 3 P.S. § 952 (1996, June 12, P.L. 336, No. 52, § 1); Nutrient Management Act, 3 P.S. §1717; *see Burkholder v. Richmond Township*, 902 A.2d 1006 (Pa.Cmwlth. 2006) (striking a municipal setback provision for factory farm manure storage facilities)); **sewage sludge** (Solid Waste Management Act, 35 P.S. § 6018.101 *et seq.*; *see Liverpool Twp v. Stephens*, 900 A.2d 1030 (Pa.Cmwlth. 2006) (striking a township's sewage sludge regulatory scheme as preempted by the SWMA, in part because the local scheme was more stringent)); **timber harvesting** (in 2000, the legislature amended the Municipalities Planning Code to make timber harvesting a "permitted use by right in all zoning districts in every municipality." 53 P.S. §10603(f)); **water withdrawal** (in 2002, the legislature removed authority from municipalities to control or regulate large water withdrawals; *see* 27 Pa.C.S. §3136(b)); **land development** (53 P.S. §10103; *see Rural Area Concerned Citizens, Inc. v. Fayette County Zoning*

Hearing Bd., 646 A.2d 717 (Pa.Cmwlth. 1994), *appeal denied*, 658 A.2d 798 (declaring that all decisions made about uses of land enacted contrary to the Municipalities Planning Code are preempted)); **hydraulic fracturing** (Act 13 of 2012, ch. 33, "Local Ordinances Relating to Oil and Gas Operation," partially overturned by the Pennsylvania Supreme Court in *Robinson Township, et al. v. Commonwealth of Pennsylvania, et al.*, 83 A.3d 901 (2013)); and **genetically modified seeds** (3 Pa.C.S. § 7120(b)), among other issues.

[59] Ironically, PGE's lawsuit against Grant Township actually *proves that the people of Grant Township were correct* – that under the traditional system of municipal governance their local government neither recognizes their self-governing authority nor is it capable of protecting and securing their civil and political rights.

[60] While it is unnecessary to the result, the U.S. Environmental Protection Agency shares the people's concern regarding pollution from the depositing of oil and gas wastes. Despite industry's claim that natural gas extraction, as regulated, does not pollute water, the federal EPA recently found that it does. *See* U.S. Environmental Protection Agency, *Investigation of Ground Water Contamination near Pavillion, Wyoming*, draft, (December, 2011), http://www.epa.gov/region8/superfund/wy/pavillion/EPA_ReportOnP avillion_Dec-8-2011.pdf (accessed November 10, 2014). In its report, the EPA concluded that both natural gas extraction wells and the related surface pits that store wastewater from the extraction process were the source of ground water contamination near Pavillion, Wyoming. With regard to the surface pits, the report said, "Detection of high concentrations of benzene, xylenes, gasoline range organics, diesel range organics, and total purgeable hydrocarbons in ground water samples from shallow monitoring wells near pits indicates that pits are a source of shallow ground water contamination in the area of investigation" *Id.* at xi. With regard to the natural gas extraction process, the report said, "Alternative explanations were carefully considered to explain individual sets of data. However, when considered together with other lines of evidence, the data indicates likely impact to ground water that can be explained by hydraulic fracturing." *Id.* at xiii.

[61] The specific part of the decision resting on the provisions of Article I, §27 of the Pennsylvania Constitution was supported by a plurality of the Pennsylvania Supreme Court.

[62] The Community Bill of Rights Ordinance secures the "right to clean air, water, and soil;" the "right to scenic preservation,"; and the rights of

ecosystems; all of which are also protected by the Pennsylvania Constitution's "right to clean air, pure water, and to the preservation of the natural, scenic, historic, and esthetic values of the environment." [Doc. 1-1 (Ordinance at §§2(a) – 2(d))].

Grant Township, Indiana County, Pennsylvania Community Bill of Rights Ordinance

Establishing a Community Bill of Rights for the People of Grant Township, Indiana County, Pennsylvania, which Prohibits Activities and Projects that would Violate the Bill of Rights, and which Provides for Enforcement of the Bill of Rights

Whereas, this community finds that the depositing of waste from oil and gas extraction is economically and environmentally unsustainable, in that it damages property values and the natural environment, and places the health of residents at risk, while failing to provide real benefits to the people of this community; and

Whereas, this community finds that the depositing of waste from oil and gas extraction violates the rights of Grant Township residents, including our right to make decisions about what happens to the places where we live; and

Whereas, private corporations engaged in the depositing of waste from oil and gas extraction are wrongly recognized by the federal and state government as having more "rights" than the people who live in our community, and thus, recognition of corporate "rights" is a denial of the rights of the people of Grant Township; and

Whereas, such denials violate the inherent right of people to local self-government; the guarantees of the Pennsylvania Constitution; and the guarantees of the Declaration of Independence and the United States Constitution; and

Whereas, the 1776 Pennsylvania Constitution recognized the inherent right of Pennsylvanians to local self-government by declaring that "all government ought to be instituted and supported for the security and protection of the community as such;" and

Whereas, that right to local self-government, now recognized and secured by Article 1, Section 2 of the current Pennsylvania Constitution, declares that "all power is inherent in the people, and all free governments are founded on their authority and instituted for their peace, safety, and happiness;" and

Whereas, this ordinance establishes a Community Bill of Rights to further recognize the right to local self-government in Grant Township, and secures that right by prohibiting those activities that would violate this local bill of rights;

Therefore, We the People of Grant Township hereby adopt this Community Bill of Rights Ordinance.

Section 1 – Definitions

(a) **"Corporations,"** for purposes of this Ordinance, shall include any corporation, limited partnership, limited liability partnership, business trust, public benefit corporation, business entity, or limited liability company organized under the laws of any state of the United States or under the laws of any country.

(b) **"Depositing of waste from oil and gas extraction"** shall include, but not be limited to, the depositing, disposal, storage, beneficial use, treatment, recycling, injection, or introduction of materials including, but not limited to, brine, "produced water," "frack water," tailings, flowback or any other waste or by-product of oil and gas extraction, by any means. The phrase shall also include the issuance of, or application for, any permit that would purport to allow these activities. This phrase shall not include temporary storage of oil and gas waste materials in the Township at existing well sites.

(c) **"Extraction"** shall mean the digging or drilling of a well for the purposes of exploring for, developing or producing shale gas, oil, or other hydrocarbons.

Section 2 – Statements of Law – A Community Bill of Rights

(a) *Right to Local Self-Government*. All residents of Grant Township possess the right to a form of governance where they live which recognizes that all power is inherent in the people and that all free governments are founded on the people's consent. Use of the municipal corporation "Grant Township" by the people for the making and enforcement of this law shall not be deemed, by any authority, to eliminate, limit, or reduce that sovereign right.

(b) *Right to Clean Air, Water and Soil*. All residents of Grant Township, along with natural communities and ecosystems within the Township, possess the right to clean air, water, and soil, which shall include the right to be free from activities which may pose potential risks to clean air, water, and soil within the Township, including the depositing of waste from oil and gas extraction.

(c) *Right to Scenic Preservation*. All residents of Grant Township possess a right to the scenic, historic and aesthetic values of the Township, including unspoiled vistas and a rural quality of life. That right shall include the right of the residents of the Township to be free from activities which threaten scenic, historic, and aesthetic values, including the depositing of waste from oil and gas extraction.

(d) *Rights of Natural Communities and Ecosystems*. Natural communities and ecosystems within Grant Township, including but not limited to, rivers, streams, and aquifers, possess the right to exist, flourish, and naturally evolve.

(e) *Right to a Sustainable Energy Future*. All residents of Grant Township possess the right to a sustainable energy future, which includes, but is not limited to, the development, production, and use of energy from renewable and sustainable fuel sources, the right to establish local sustainable energy policies to further secure this right, and the right to be free from energy extraction, production, and use that may adversely impact the rights of human or natural communities. That right shall include the right to be free from activities related to fossil fuel extraction and production, including the depositing of waste from oil and gas extraction.

(f) *Right to Enforce.* All residents of Grant Township possess the right to enforce the rights and prohibitions secured by this Ordinance, which shall include the right of Township residents to intervene in any legal action involving the rights and prohibitions of this Ordinance.

(g) *Rights as Self-Executing.* All rights delineated and secured by this Ordinance are inherent, fundamental, and unalienable, and shall be self-executing and enforceable against both private and public actors. The rights secured by this Ordinance shall only be enforceable against actions specifically prohibited by this Ordinance.

Section 3 – Statements of Law – Prohibitions Necessary to Secure the Bill of Rights

(a) It shall be unlawful within Grant Township for any corporation or government to engage in the depositing of waste from oil and gas extraction.

(b) No permit, license, privilege, charter, or other authority issued by any state or federal entity which would violate the prohibitions of this Ordinance or any rights secured by this Ordinance, the Pennsylvania Constitution, the United States Constitution, or other laws, shall be deemed valid within Grant Township.

Section 4 – Enforcement

(a) Any corporation or government that violates any provision of this Ordinance shall be guilty of an offense and, upon conviction thereof, shall be sentenced to pay the maximum fine allowable under State law for that violation. Each day or portion thereof, and violation of each section of this Ordinance, shall count as a separate violation.

(b) Grant Township, or any resident of the Township, may enforce the rights and prohibitions of this Ordinance through an action brought in any court possessing jurisdiction over activities occurring within the Township. In such an action, the Township or the resident shall be entitled to recover all costs of litigation, including, without limitation, expert and attorney's fees.

(c) Any action brought by either a resident of Grant Township or by the Township to enforce or defend the rights of ecosystems or natural communities secured by this Ordinance shall bring that action in the name of the ecosystem or natural community in a court possessing jurisdiction over activities occurring within the Township. Damages shall be measured by the cost of restoring the ecosystem or natural community to its state before the injury, and shall be paid to the Township to be used exclusively for the full and complete restoration of the ecosystem or natural community.

Section 5 – Enforcement – Corporate Powers

(a) Corporations that violate this Ordinance, or that seek to violate this Ordinance, shall not be deemed to be "persons," nor possess any other legal rights, privileges, powers, or protections which would interfere with the rights or prohibitions enumerated by this Ordinance. "Rights, privileges, powers, or protections" shall include the power to assert state or federal preemptive laws in an attempt to overturn this Ordinance, and the power to assert that the people of this municipality lack the authority to adopt this Ordinance.

(b) All laws adopted by the legislature of the State of Pennsylvania, and rules adopted by any State agency, shall be the law of Grant Township only to the extent that they do not violate the rights or prohibitions of this Ordinance.

Section 6 – Effective Date and Existing Permit Holders

This Ordinance shall be effective immediately on the date of its enactment, at which point the Ordinance shall apply to any and all actions that would violate this Ordinance, regardless of the date of any applicable local, state, or federal permit.

Section 7 – People's Right to Self-Government

Use of the courts or the Pennsylvania legislature in attempts to overturn the provisions of this Ordinance shall require community meetings focused on changes to local governance that would secure the right of the people to local self-government.

Section 8 – State and Federal Constitutional Changes

Through the adoption of this Ordinance, the people of Grant Township call for amendment of the Pennsylvania Constitution and the federal Constitution to recognize a right to local self-government free from governmental preemption and or nullification by corporate "rights."

Section 9 – Severability

The provisions of this Ordinance are severable. If any court decides that any section, clause, sentence, part, or provision of this Ordinance is illegal, invalid, or unconstitutional, such decision shall not affect, impair, or invalidate any of the remaining sections, clauses, sentences, parts, or provisions of the Ordinance.

Section 10 – Repealer

All inconsistent provisions of prior Ordinances adopted by Grant Township are hereby repealed, but only to the extent necessary to remedy the inconsistency.